CONTROLLING COLOR

Controlling Color

A PRACTICAL INTRODUCTION FOR DESIGNERS AND ARTISTS

Patricia Lambert

DESIGN PRESS

First Edition, First Printing

Printed in Hong Kong by Everbest Printing Company Ltd.
Designed by Ann Gold

Library of Congress Cataloging-in-Publication Data
Lambert, Patricia.
Controlling color : a practical introduction for designers and artists / Patricia Lambert.
p. cm.
Includes index.
ISBN 0-8306-3559-9 : $16.60
1. Color. I. Title.
QC495.L248 1991
701′.85—dc20 90-21603
CIP

Questions regarding the content of this book should be addressed to:

Design Press
11 West 19th Street
New York, NY 10011

Design Press books are published by Design Press, an imprint of TAB Books. TAB Books is a Division of McGraw-Hill, Inc.

For Lynn, Simbah, Otto, and their friends,
all very special teachers

ACKNOWLEDGMENTS

I would like to express my gratitude to the following people for their time, talents, and expertise in the preparation of this book: my students at the Parsons School of Design, especially Phyllis Mulholland, Lena Vilhjalmsson, Dianne Wenz, I-Wen Tseng, David Ye, and Heather Eatman; Betty Chen Louis; Steven Gray; Nancy Green and Gina Webster at Design Press; and the book designer, Ann Gold. I am particularly grateful to my assistant, Michael Sullivan, and to Frederica Paine for her endurance, support, and inspired illustrations.

Design Variations in Value

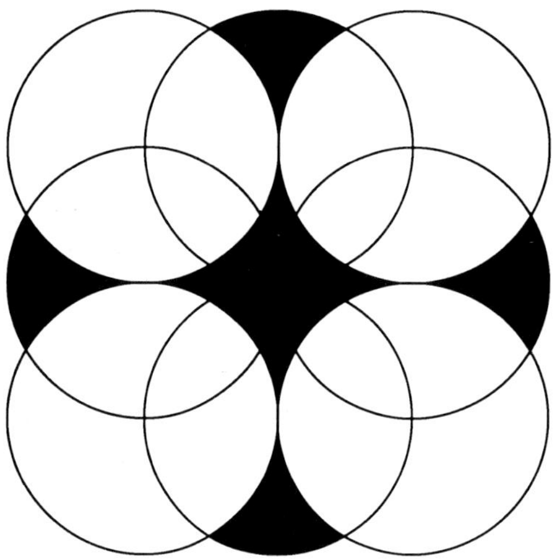

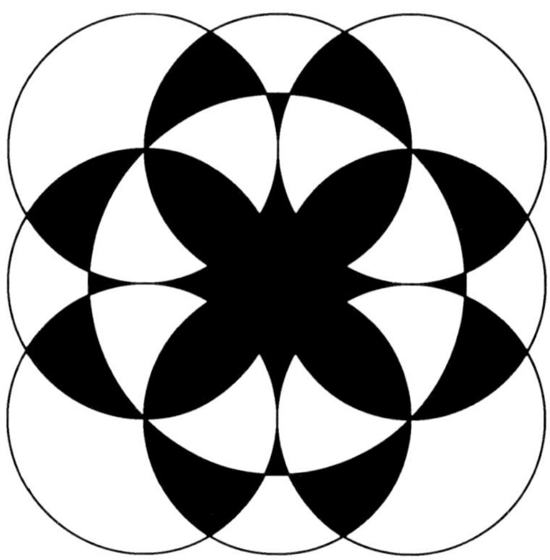

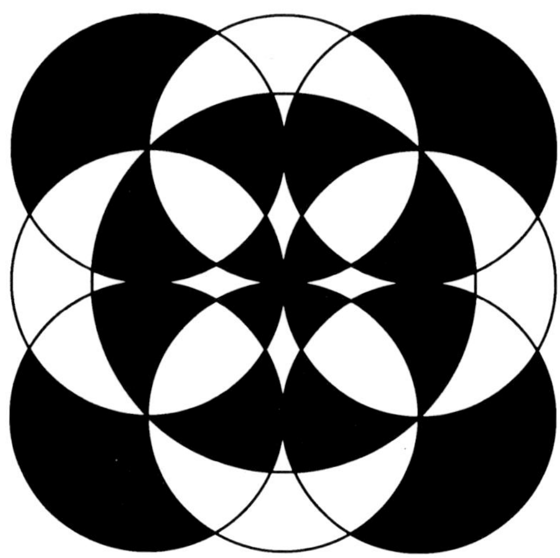

PREFACE

A journey of a thousand miles
starts under one's feet.
—Lao Tsu

It may appear strange to introduce a contemporary text about color with an ancient Taoist thought, but nothing is more appropriate. My own sense of journey began while I was trying to solve color problems without taking the time to study the subject. Seeing my frustration at wanting to get on with the actual work, an artist friend suggested that the process of learning to control color is a lifetime journey, needing a balance of intellect and intuition as one progresses step by step. I was operating from an intuitive sense alone, and not getting very far. Color problems often can be resolved in a simple intuitive way, but using intuition alone is like working in a house with no foundation. It may hold up for a little while, but soon it becomes unsteady and before long comes crashing down. The paradox is that the more you learn, the better your intuition functions.

Controlling Color is intended to help designers and artists begin that integration of intuition, thought, study, and application, all of which are necessary to progress. It has also been my experience that without a balance of the practical and the theoretical, original work cannot flourish.

As a practicing artist, teacher, and theorist, I am deeply involved with color both aesthetically and spiritually. It is my sincere wish that this book provide an underpinning of color information and become a first step for many creative journeys.

Design Variations in Value

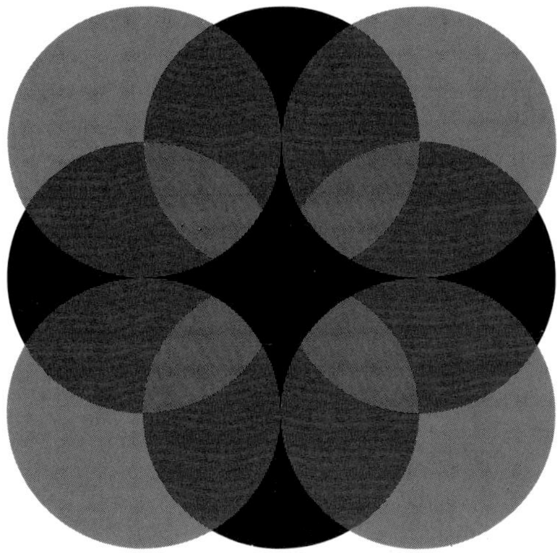

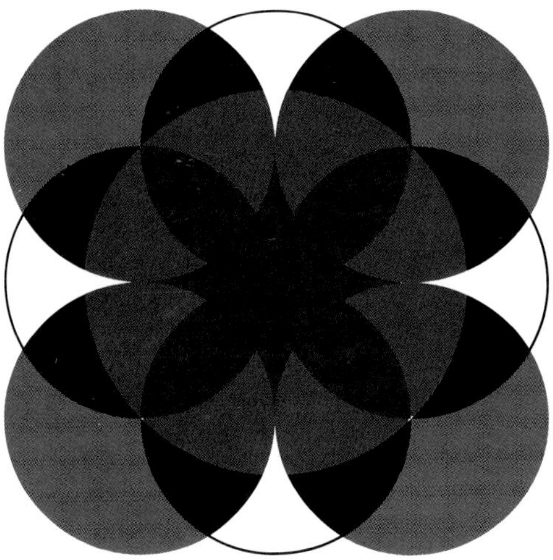

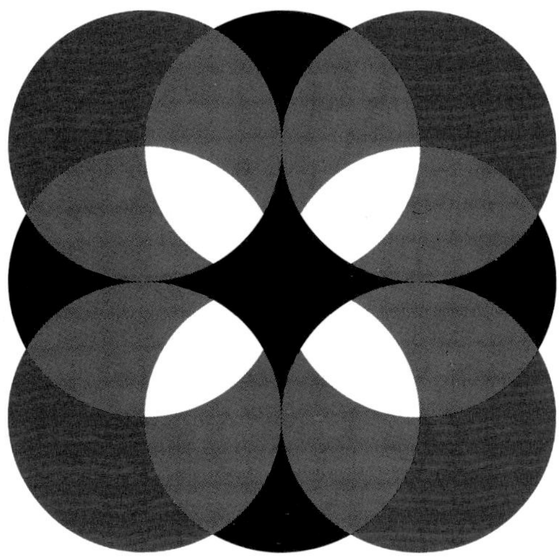

ILLUSTRATION CREDITS

All illustrations are by Frederica Paine except as follows:

Page 10	Haruetai Muodtong
Figure 2-4	Phyllis Mulholland and Michael Sullivan
Figure 2-6	Michael Sullivan
Figure 3-1	Michael Sullivan
Figures 3-4 – 3-6	David Ye
Figure 3-8	Michael Sullivan
Figures 4-1 – 4-5	Barbara Jaffe
Figure 4-6	I-Wen Tseng
Figures 4-11 – 4-13	Barbara Jaffe
Figure 4-15	Dianne Wenz
Figure 4-25	Lena Vilhjalmsson
Figures 5-1 – 5-3	Heather Eatman
Figure 5-4	David Ye
Figure 5-5	Phyllis Mulholland
Figures 5-6, 5-7	David Ye
Figure 5-8	Michael Sullivan
Figures 5-9, 5-10	David Ye

Design Variations in Value

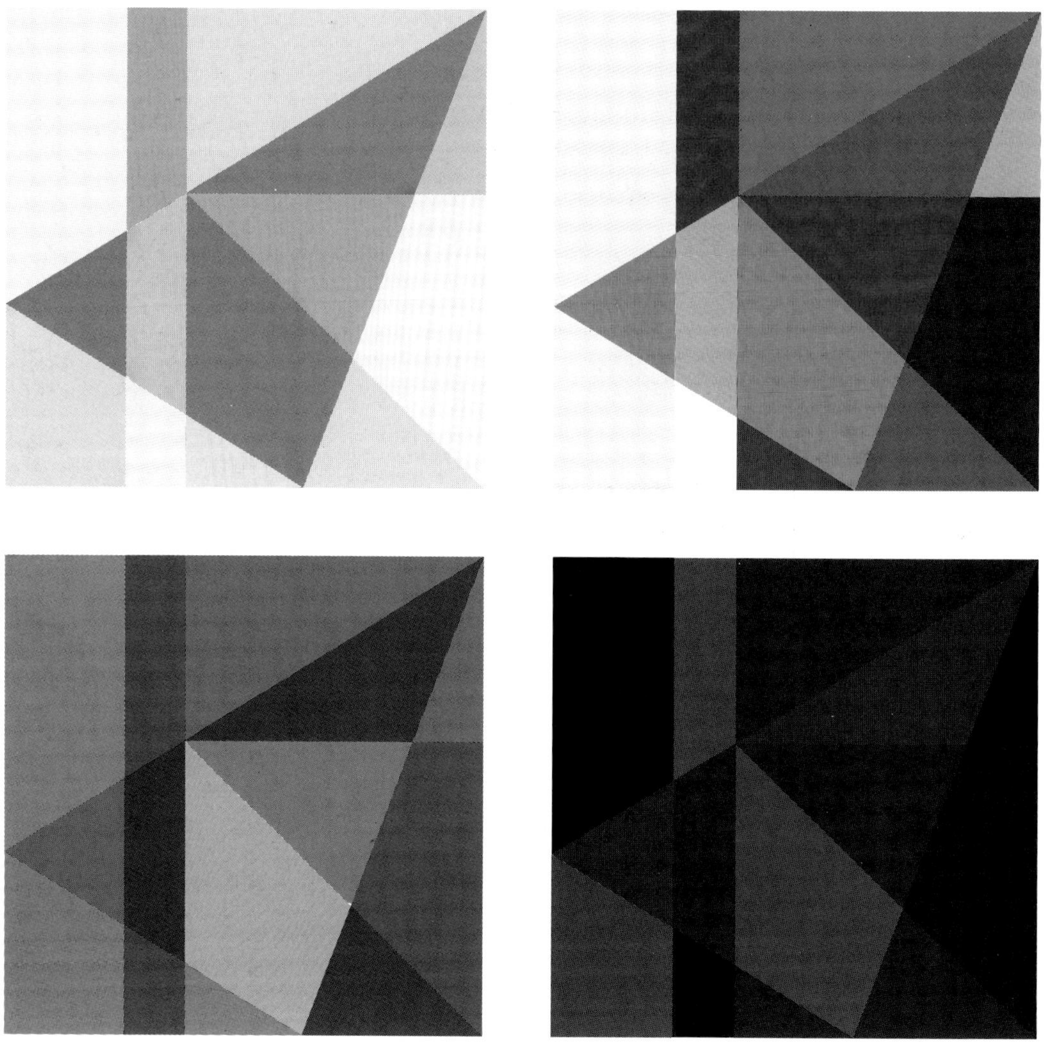

CONTENTS

1 COLOR: ORIGINS AND SOURCES

Radiation

The tremendous forces produced by galaxies, stars, and other cosmic phenomena create radiant energy that penetrates the earth's atmosphere. Although we live in the midst of this vast ocean of radiation and are profoundly affected by it, it remains, for the most part invisible to us. This energy, or electromagnetic radiation, travels in a wave motion that closely resembles the motion of ripples on a pond or waves breaking at a beach. The waves of radiation can travel through space and atmosphere at almost any frequency—the number of complete waves or cycles that pass a given point in 1 second (figure 1-1). A great variety of frequencies and *wavelengths* make up the great electromagnetic spectrum (figure 1-2), ranging from radio and power waves miles in length to cosmic rays or waves that measure as little as 0.000000000000394 inch.

Visible Light

Although we are aware of all kinds of electromagnetic radiation through its effects on our bodies and on the environment (figure 1-3) the human eye is only sensitive to the very narrow portion of the continuum called *light*. The wavelengths of electromagnetic radiation, including light, are generally measured in nanometers (nm). Since 1 nm is equivalent to 1 billionth of a meter (which is itself equal to about 39.37 inches), the lengths involved are not at all detectable as individual wavelengths. The wavelengths of light measure from 400 to 700nm. This section of the great spectrum is usually referred to as *visible light* or the *visible light spectrum*.

It is generally agreed that the first experiments establishing today's color science were performed by the physical scientist and mathematician Sir Isaac Newton in 1676. He had the idea that visible light, or white light, was actually made up of a series of individual colors. Possibly stimulated by the general scientific interest in light and lenses, Newton

Figure 1-1 Waves of Electromagnetic Radiation

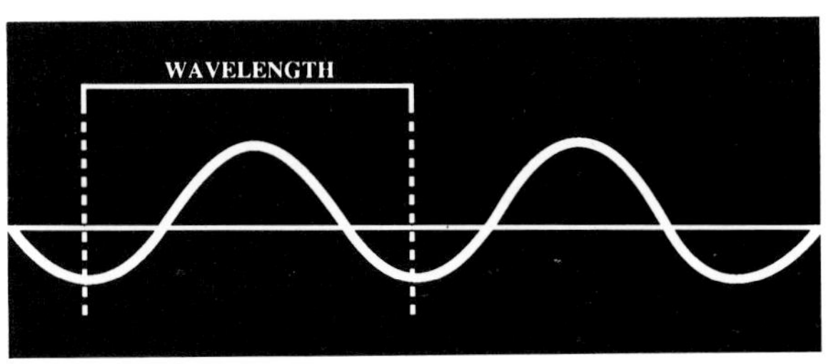

devised a now-classic experiment consisting of a beam of light aimed at a triangular piece of glass called a prism and a projection screen. The light beam is bent (or refracted) and spread before projecting onto a white screen or surface (figure 1-4). Although scientists offered various explanations for the prism effect, Newton determined that the white light itself was actually made up of these colored bands, which he called the *visible spectrum*. The colored bands are called *spectral hues* and have specific wavelengths. Red is refracted the least and has the longest wavelength (up to 700 nm), while blue is refracted the most and has the shortest wavelength (as little as 400nm).

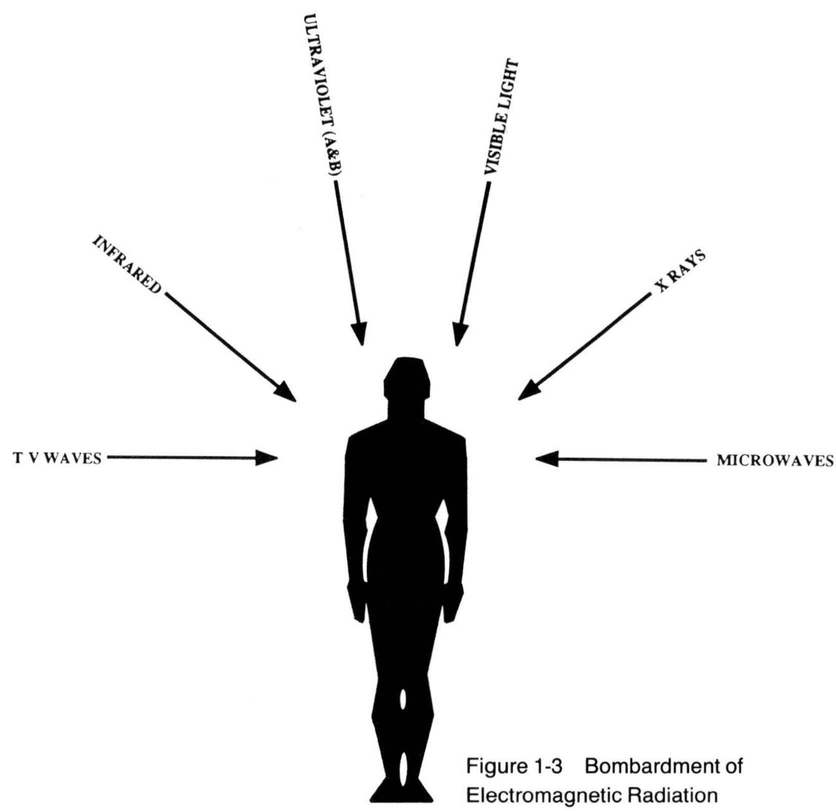

Figure 1-3 Bombardment of Electromagnetic Radiation

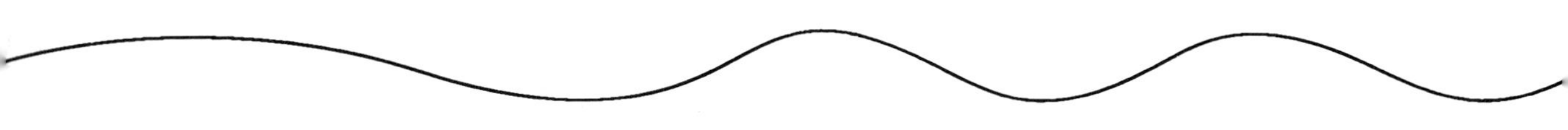

Figure 1-2 Electromagnetic Spectrum

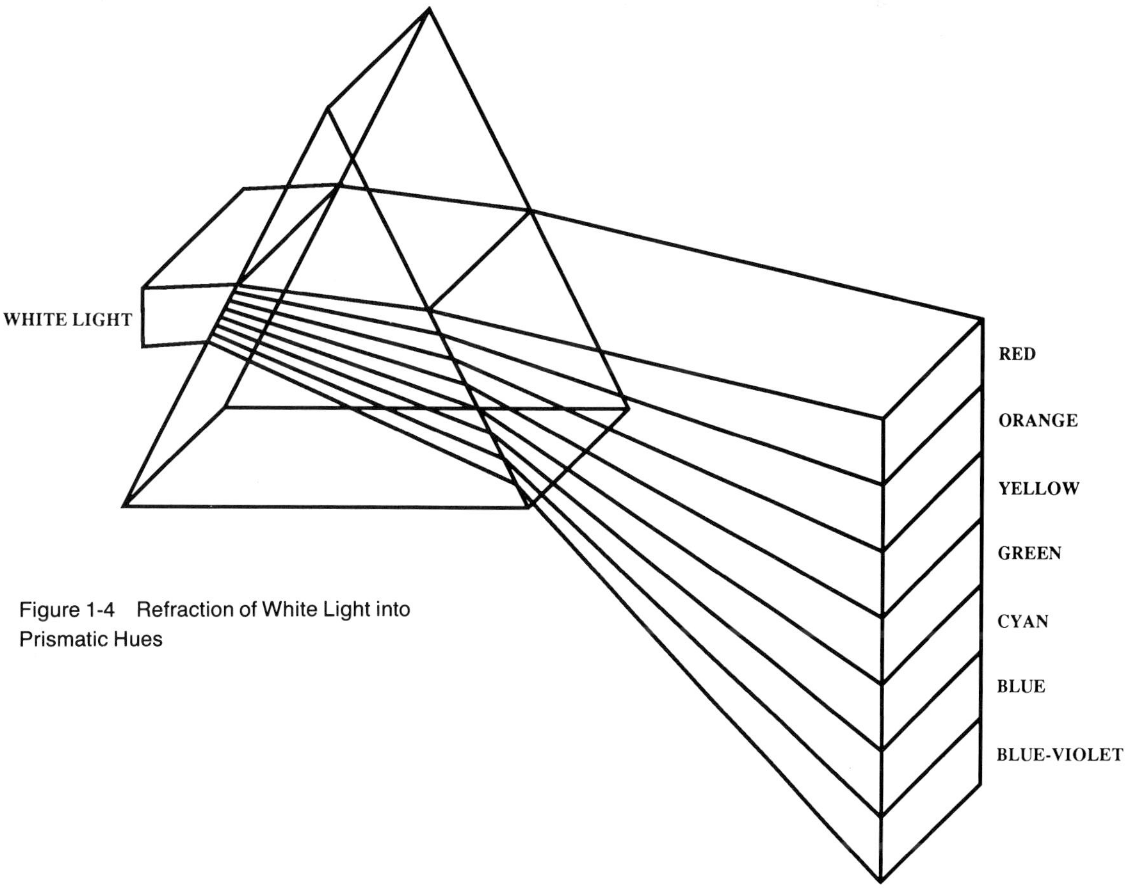

Figure 1-4 Refraction of White Light into Prismatic Hues

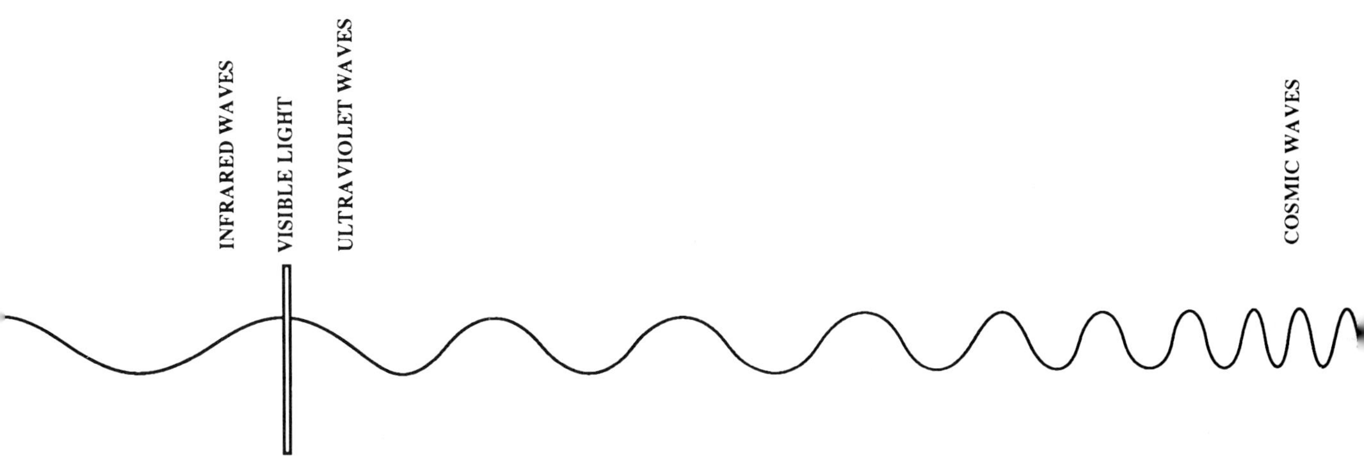

Additive Mixing

The largest areas of color seen in the visible spectrum are red-orange (RO), green (G), and blue-violet (BV) (figure 1-5). These three spectral hues are known as the *light primaries*. When each light primary is projected singly and overlapped (figure 1-6a – b), the combination of any two hues forms a secondary hue. The mixture of RO and BV produces magenta (M); RO and G produces yellow (Y); and BV and G produces cyan (C). Each secondary is lighter than the two parent primaries. The final product of all three primaries, or of a primary and an unrelated secondary hue (the same thing) is white light (figure 1-6c). This process of adding wavelengths of light together to make other colors or to produce white light is called *additive mixing*.

If the visible spectrum is curved into a circle, the relationship between primary and secondary hues becomes apparent (figure 1-7). Each primary lies opposite a secondary, and together these are known as *complementary* pairs because when combined they produce white light. The only color that is not monochromatic—that is, does not have a single measurable wavelength (and indeed, does not exist in the spectrum)—is magenta. Magenta is only seen when the long wavelengths of red are combined with the short wavelengths of blue; it is thus an interesting result of seeing the visible spectrum as a circle.

Colorants

The term *colorant* refers to any substance that causes a color change in or on another substance. There are many different kinds of colorants, both organic (such as plant and animal material) and inorganic (including mineral and gemstone colorants, as well as synthetic dyes and pigments). Some colorants yield striking effects, such as fluorescent brighteners, metallic additives, and pearlescent and luminescent material containing mica and mineral impurities; but the most common colorants are dyes and pigments (paints) plus a variety of transparent and translucent material like acetate sheets, glass, and fabric that are of particular concern to the artist.

The principle difference between dyes and pigments is solubility. Most dyes are soluble or can be made soluble in a liquid medium and have the characteristic of staining a surface after penetrating it to some degree. All pigments are insoluble in the medium in which they are suspended and usually require a gluey substance or binder to hold them to the substrate—the ground or support onto which they are brushed or sprayed (figure 1-8). Inks are most often a combination of dyes and pigments.

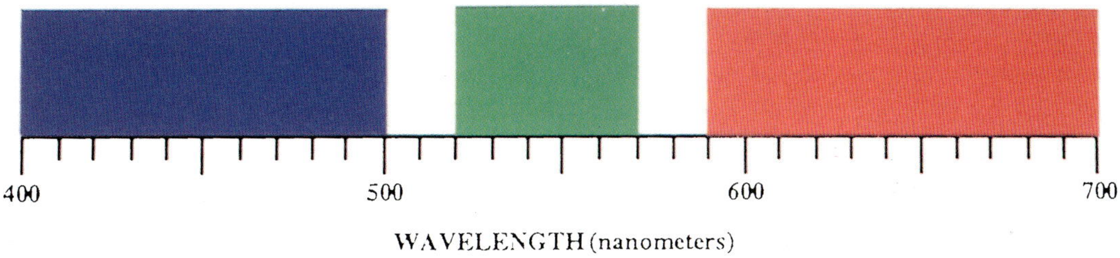

Figure 1-5 Light Primaries

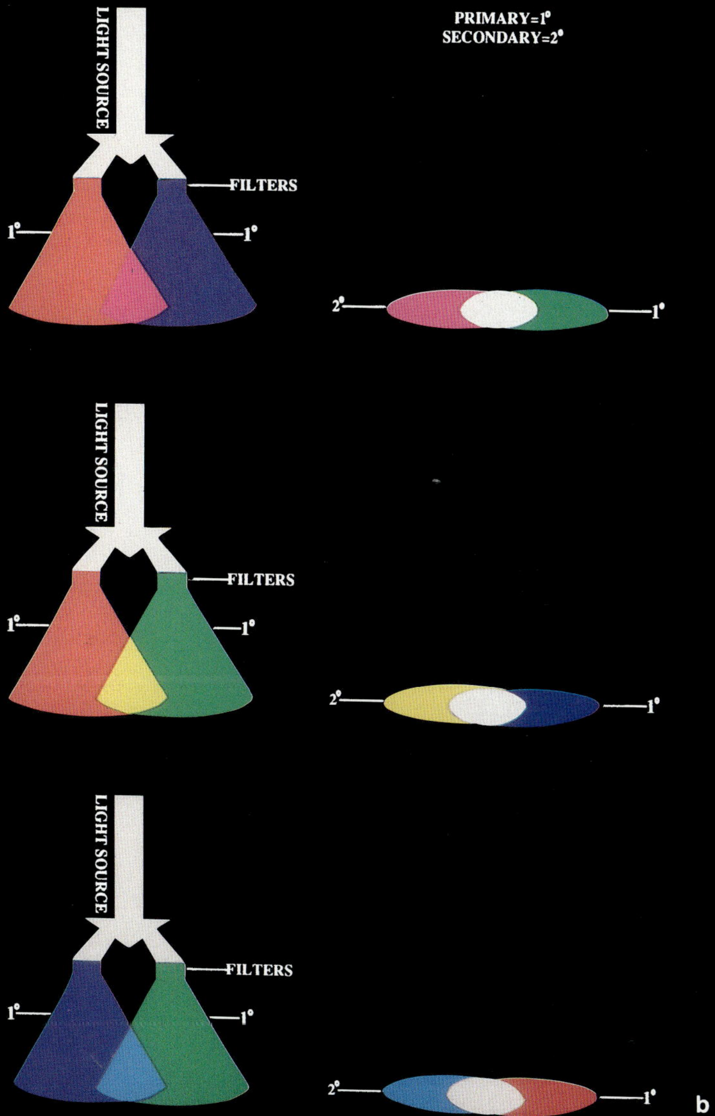

igure 1-6 Additive Mixing:
a) Two light primaries produce a
ght secondary; (b) A light
rimary plus a light secondary
roduce white light; (c) All three
ght primaries produce white
ght; (d) Filters of the light
econdary hues work in the
pposite way to additive mixing;
hey become the true subtractive
r pigment primaries and
ombine to produce black.

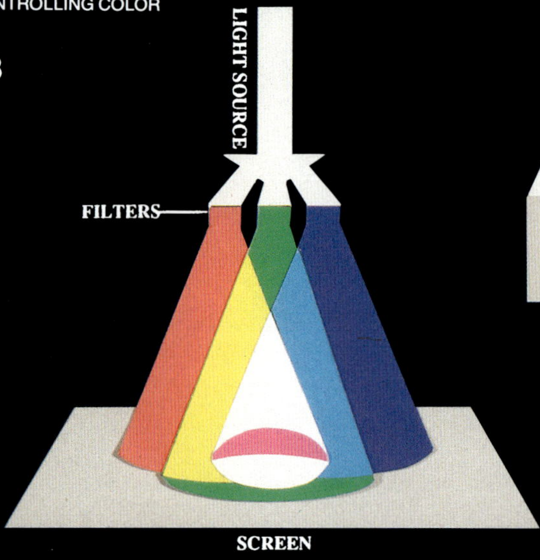

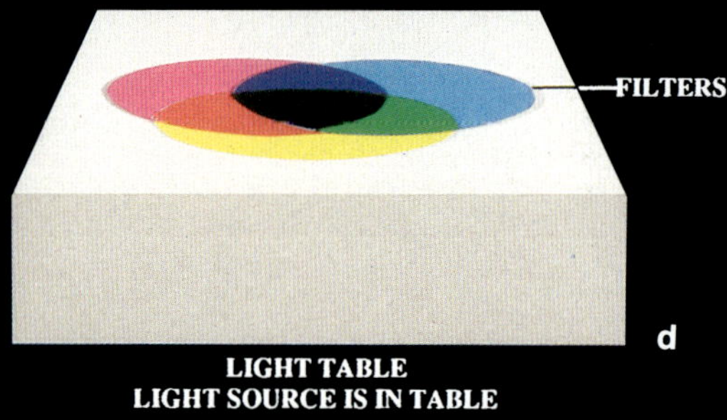

Figure 1-6 (continued)

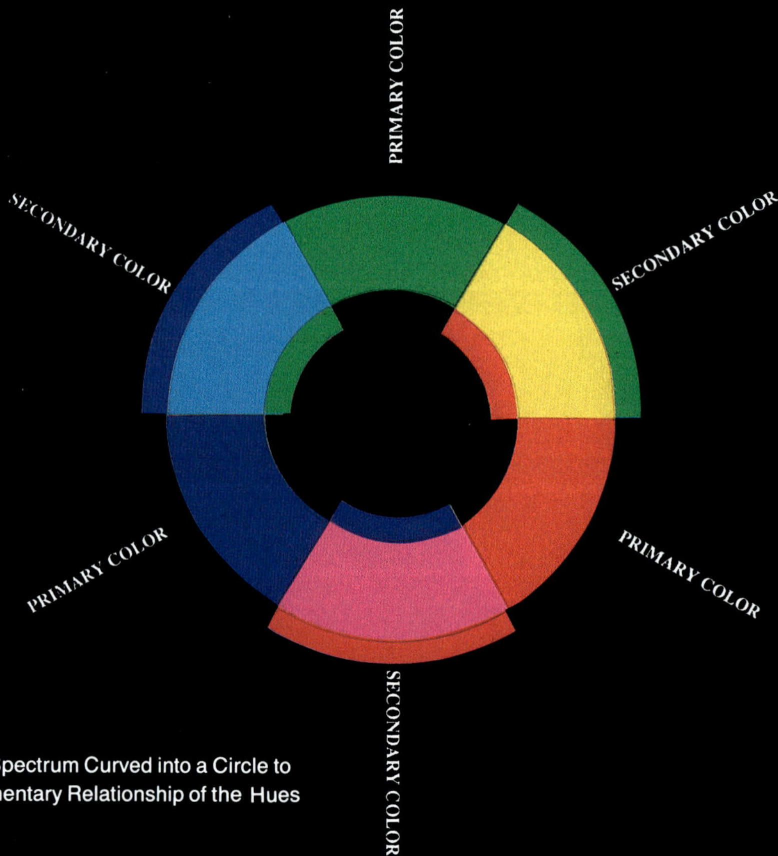

Figure 1-7 Light Spectrum Curved into a Circle to Show the Complementary Relationship of the Hues

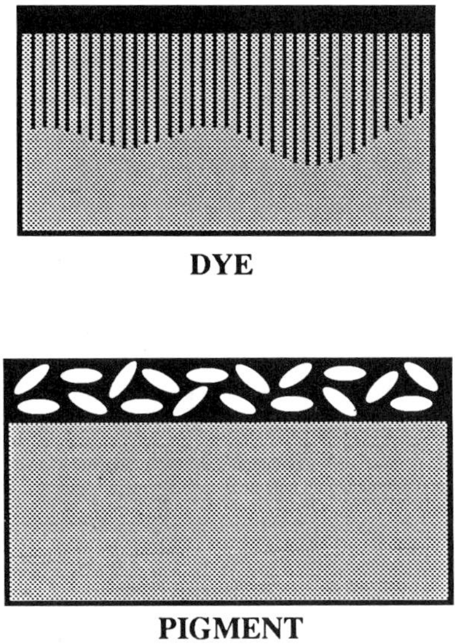

Figure 1-8 Solubility of Colorant to Substrate

Subtractive Mixing

When paints, inks, and dyes are mixed or when colored translucent material is layered as in figure 1-6d, the resulting mixtures are said to be *subtractive*. For example, when a beam of white light passes through a filter of a specific color, only the wavelength of light that is the same color as the filter is transmitted (figure 1-9a). All of the other colors in the white light are absorbed into the filter and thus subtracted out of the beam. Now consider what happens when white light passes through a series of three filters; one yellow, one magenta, and one cyan (figure 1-9b). The first filter, yellow, will allow the red-orange and green wavelengths through it, but will absorb the blue wavelengths. The next filter, magenta, will allow only the red-orange component of the yellow light to be transmitted, while absorbing the green. The last filter, cyan, will absorb the remaining red-orange wavelengths, so *no light* will be transmitted. For this reason, magenta, yellow, and cyan are the true subtractive primaries. The light secondaries thus become the pigment primaries.

The process of subtractive mixing is the result of selective absorption, transmission, and/or reflection depending on the surface and colorant used. For example, when a blue paint, dye, or ink is mixed with a yellow colorant of the same material, or when blue and yellow pieces of transparent material such as glass or acetate sheeting are overlaid, the resultant color is a green whose specific character is the result of the quantity and quality of each of the parent colors used. The subtractive nature of the mixture can be easily and accurately theorized (figure 1-10). A blue colorant absorbs red and orange wavelengths of light, as well as most green wavelengths, and reflects blue wavelengths. Some green is reflected, but the blue dominates and the viewer perceives blue. Similarly, yellow absorbs the blue and blue-violet wavelengths and reflects the red and green portions of the spectrum, producing the sensation of yellow. Some true yellow is also reflected but the quantity of such wavelengths is so small as to be negligible. When the blue and yellow colorants are mixed, they cancel (subtract) each other's characteristic wavelengths; only the green wavelengths remain unabsorbed and are reflected back to be perceived as the color green.

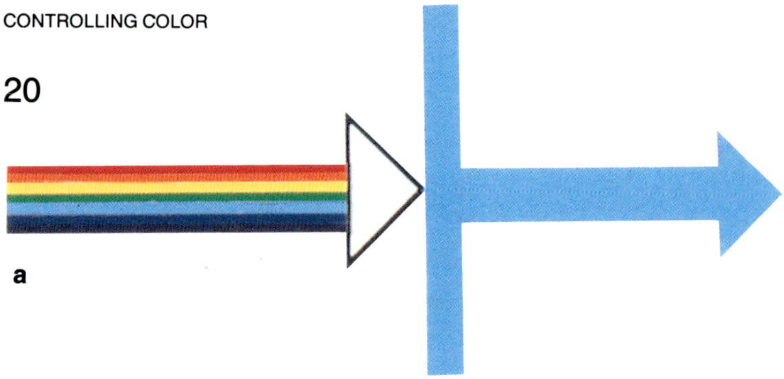

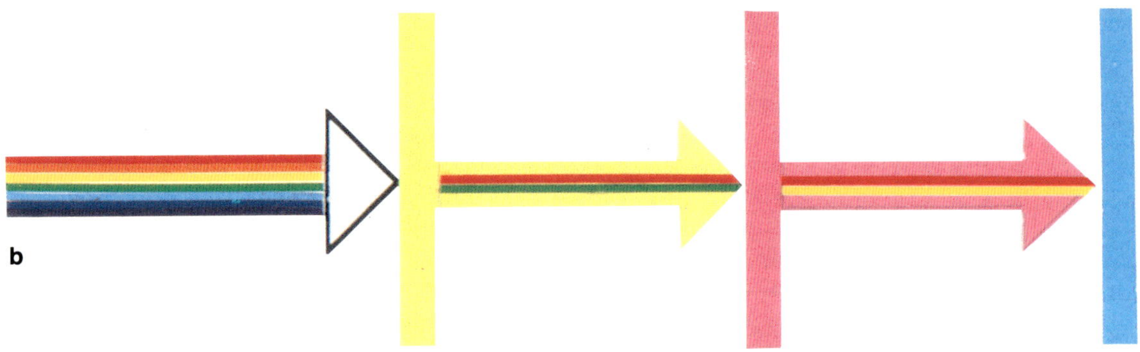

Figure 1-9 Transmission of Light Through Magenta, Yellow, and Cyan Filters: (a) Use of a single filter; (b) Use of all three filters.

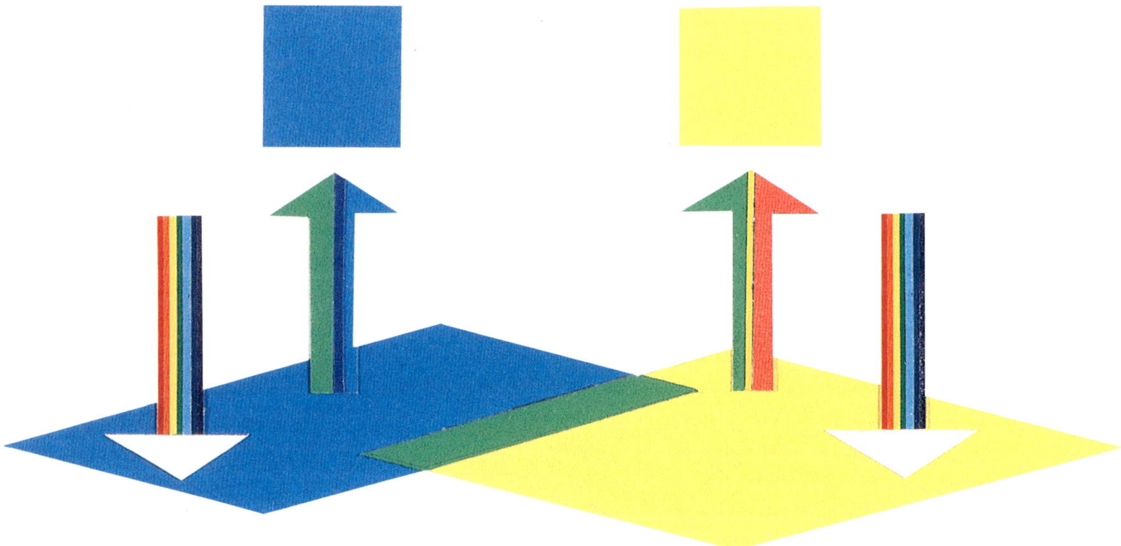

Figure 1-10 Subtractive Nature of Mixtures

Surfaces

The perceived (reflected) color of a surface is influenced by three things: the character of the surface (its roughness or smoothness); the color quality of the illumination hitting the surface; and the quantity and angle of that illumination.

Whenever light moves from one medium (such as air) to another (such as a paint film on a canvas or paper), several things happen simultaneously (figure 1-11). Some of the light is reflected back at the interface, some is absorbed, and some may be transmitted (if the material allows transmission).

If the surface is smooth, the angle at which the light is reflected will be equal to the angle at which the light hits the surface, also known as the angle of incidence (figure 1-12). This is called *specular reflection*. The light has neither penetrated very far into the surface nor had the opportunity to be reflected in many different directions by pigment particles. The color of a smooth or *glossy* surface usually conveys a feeling of more intense color except when reflecting light directly back at the viewer. At these times the color all but disappears, and glare areas or hotspots interfere with color perception; here, the angle of incidence and the angle of reflection are virtually the same (figure 1-13).

If the surface is rough or highly textured, light is reflected in a scattered or *diffuse* way (figure 1-14). Moreover, if light penetrates a paint film deeply and is reflected by many

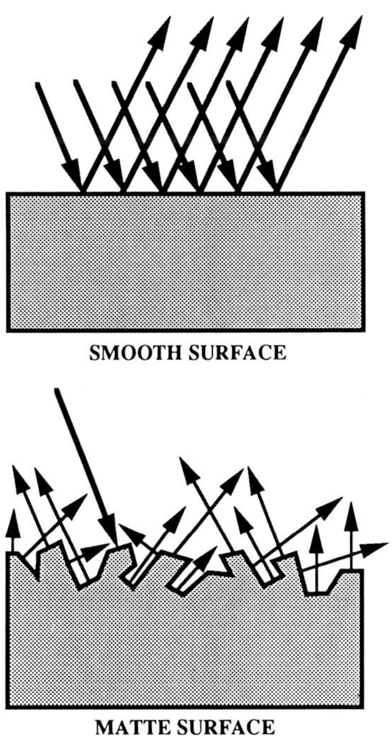

Figure 1-11 Reflection of Light on Smooth and Matte Surfaces

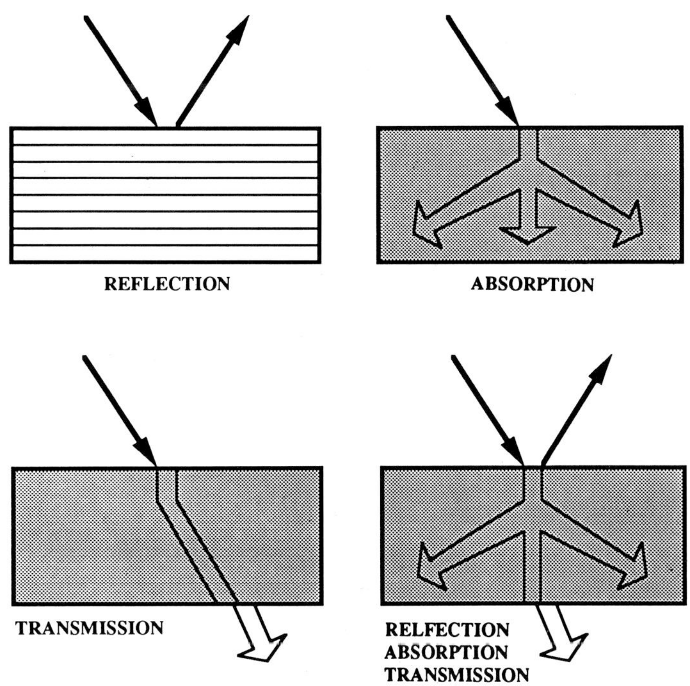

Figure 1-12 Types of Light and Surface Interaction

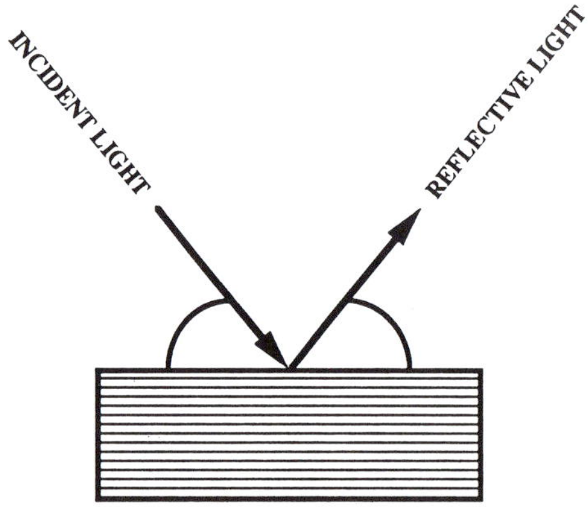

Figure 1-13 Specular Reflection

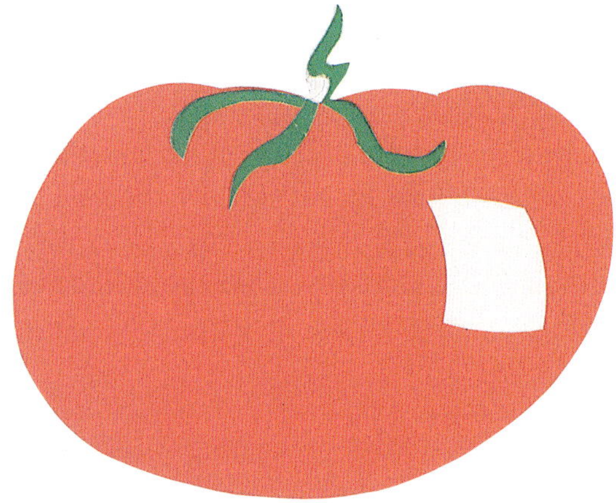

Figure 1-14 Glare Area Where Little or No Color Appears

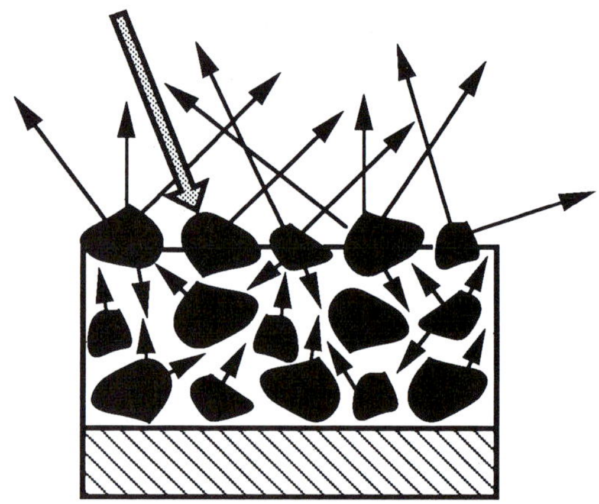

Figure 1-15 Light Diffusion

paint particles, this adds to the diffused reflection. When this happens, the reflected light is more affected by selective absorption at the surface, with less intensity or strength of color seen as a result—just the opposite of what happens with a smooth surface.

A surface that is textured and diffuses light to any degree is called *matte*. The degree of specular reflection determines the difference between a matte surface and a smooth or glossy surface (figure 1-15). For example, a glossy paint is manufactured with a suspension medium that forms a hard, smooth paint film; matte paints form films that have irregular surfaces. In painting and design, the texture of a surface may be suggested by the contrast of brightness or purity and dullness or impurity of a color. Highlights painted into an area can suggest specular reflection or smoothness, which gives the illusion of form. Varnishing a work, running water over the surface of a rock, and spreading a thin film of wax over a surface are all examples of transforming a surface from irregular to smooth and thereby enhancing its color.

Color Temperature

The *color temperature* of a light source can have an enormous influence on the way a reflected color is seen. For example, a red surface will appear cooler—that is, less red in

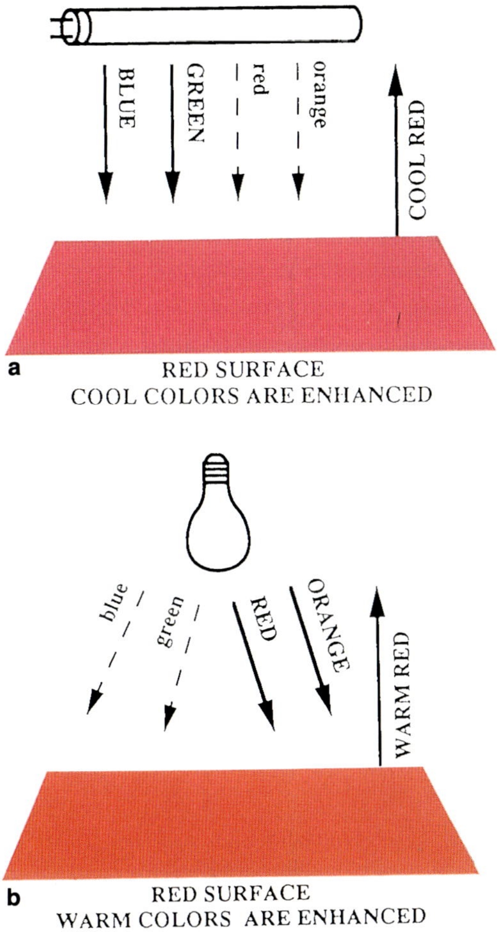

Figure 1-16 Effects of Lighting on Color Temperature: (a) Cool colors are enhanced by cool fluorescent light; (b) Warm colors are enhanced by warm tungsten light.

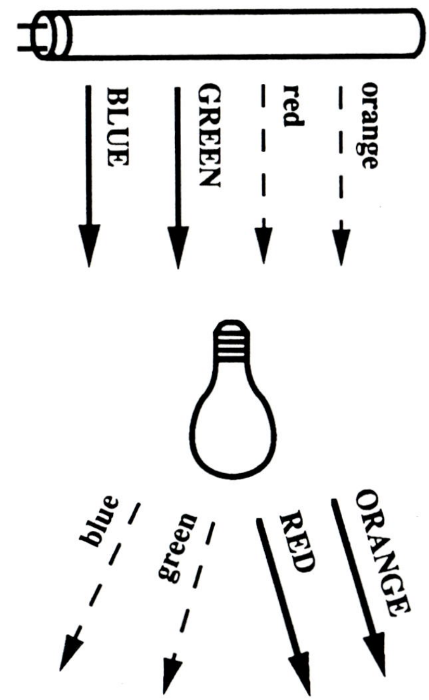

Figure 1-17 Color Dominance in Light Sources

feeling, or bluer—under a cool fluorescent light than under a regular tungsten household light bulb (figure 1-16). Since reflected color is seen by spectral reflection, the wavelength of light that the colorant reflects must be present in the spectrum that illuminates the surface. If the wavelength of light is not present—even if the colorant is specific (such as red or blue)—the surface color will not be seen to full advantage and perhaps will not be seen at all.

Neither fluorescent nor tungsten light contains all the wavelengths of visible light in the same proportion as daylight. Only in daylight or in light simulating daylight, such as full-spectrum fluorescent tubes (readily available on the market), will an accurate reading of all colors be possible because of a balanced presence of all visible wavelengths. The cool fluorescent light has a dominance of wavelengths in the blue and green portions of the visible spectrum and falls off in the red and orange end, while the tungsten light is just the opposite (figure 1-17). If a wavelength of light is not present in the light that illuminates a surface, it cannot be reflected. Thus, if a red piece of paper is lit only with green light in a darkened room, the perceived color of the red paper cannot be red (figure 1-18). Since no red wavelength is available to be reflected from the colorant, the color red is simply not perceived; only a gray having the same total light reflectance will be seen.

With this in mind, it is ideal to illuminate a color with a light source that contains similar wavelengths as the colorant. Warm colors seem warmer under tungsten lighting; cool colors more intense under cool fluorescence. Controlling the color temperature of a light source for working or exhibiting becomes an important issue for maximizing color relationships (figure 1-19).

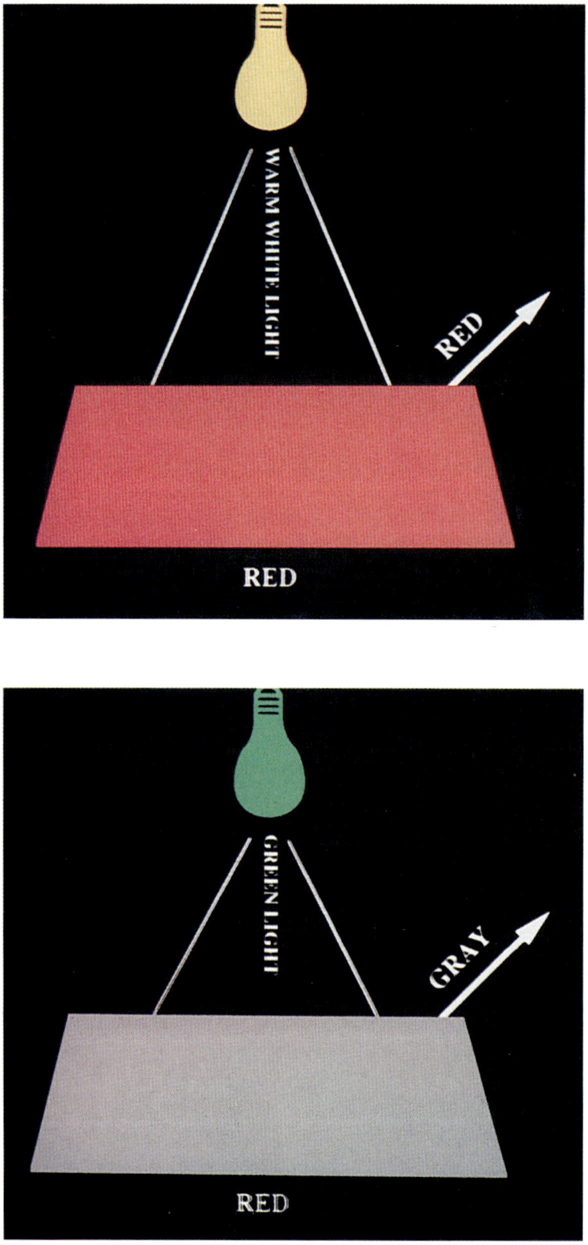

Figure 1-18 Effect of Having No Red Wavelength in Light Hitting a Red Surface

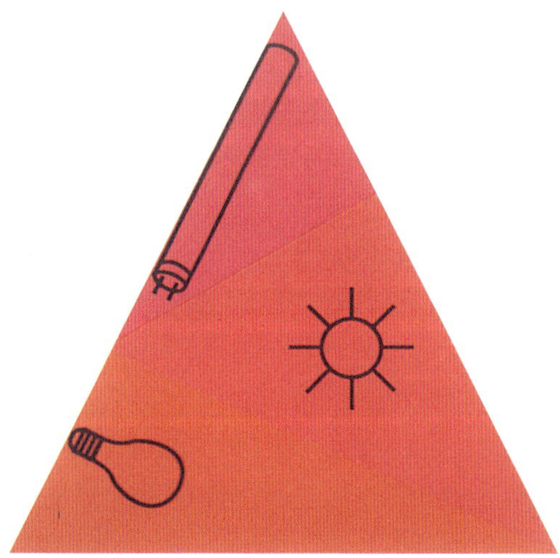

Figure 1-19 Light Source and Color Effect on Warm Colors

The quantity of illumination on a subject also affects perceived color. If a single lamp is used, the proportion of specular reflection to diffuse reflection is quite different from what it would be if many lamps were used. For this reason, many lamps on a glossy surface will dull the color, whereas a single lamp on a matte surface will make the color appear richer.

Color Constancy

The color temperature of light and its level of intensity change constantly throughout a 24-hour period. It would be reasonable to speculate that, as the light changes, our perception of color changes accordingly. Fortunately, however, it does not; life would be chaotic if it did. A white pitcher will be perceived as white whether it is seen under candlelight (which is very warm) or in daylight. An apple will be perceived as red whether it is seen under tungsten light or fluorescent light. This aspect of perception is called *color constancy* and is most probably involved with color memory, permitting us some visual stability. The trained viewer knows, however, that color shifts do occur. These shifts are most apparent when comparisons are made simultaneously; and for optimum color control, full-spectrum lighting is recommended.

2 COLOR PROPERTIES

Reflected Color

Every reflected color exhibits four basic properties: a selective spectral reflectance, or *hue* (refer to Chapter 1, figure 1-10); a percentage of totally reflected or absorbed light, or *value* (figure 2-1); a degree of reflected purity, or *intensity* (figure 2-2); and a feeling of warmness and/or coolness, or *temperature* (figure 2-3).

Just as a conductor can control the dynamics of an orchestra by understanding the characteristics of the instruments and their relationship to one another and to the score, so the visual artist can control the dynamics of color expression in a work by understanding the interactions of the four properties of color and, in turn, the relationships of the colors themselves to one another.

Hue

The words *hue* and *color* are often used interchangeably. However, *color* refers generally to any sensation the viewer receives in connection with a color. In contrast, *hue* is far more specific and has two definitions. First, *hue* may refer to the quality of a color that identifies it—that is, to its selective spectral reflection, such

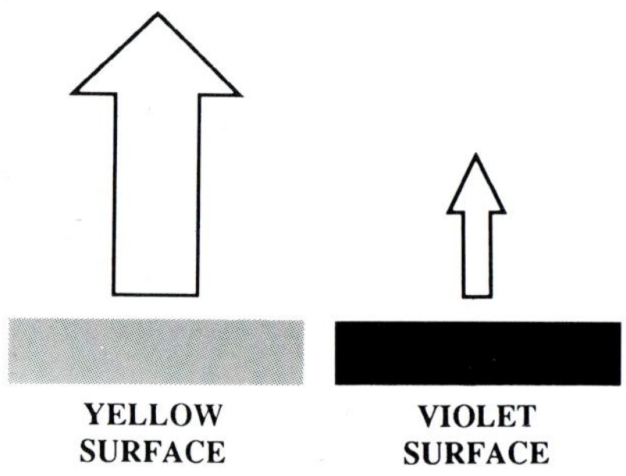

Figure 2-1 Value or Totally Reflected Light: Yellow reflects more total light than violet.

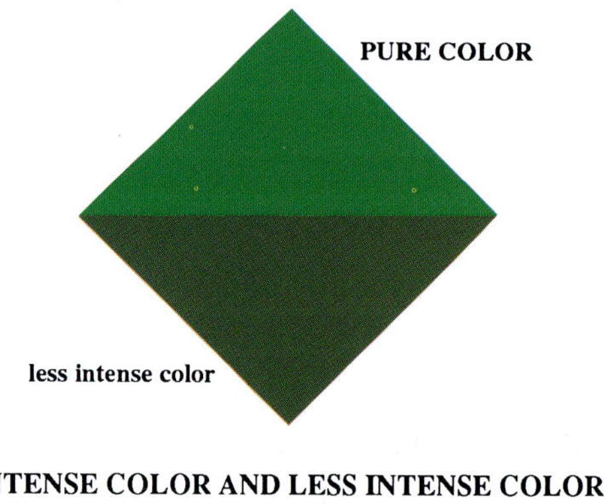

Figure 2-2 Intensity: Pure color and less intense color.

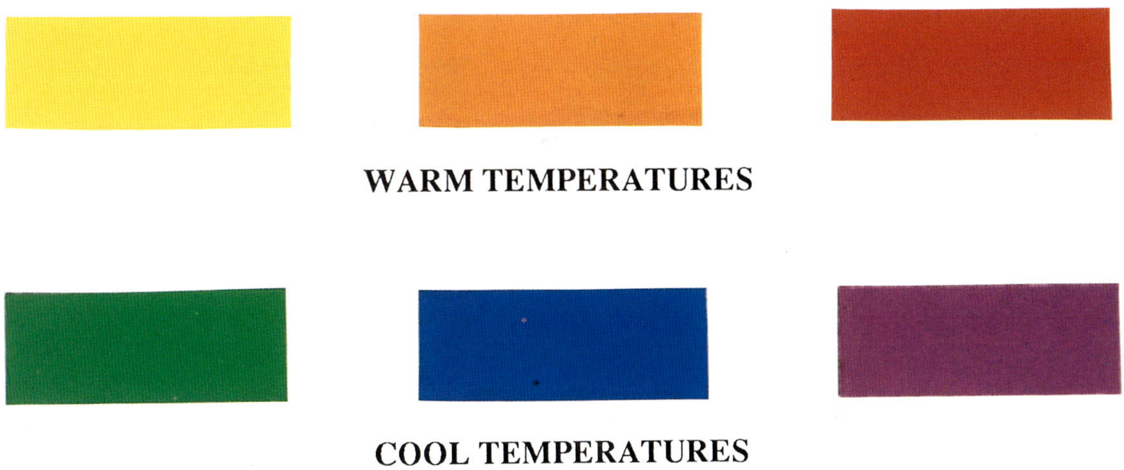

Figure 2-3 Warm and Cool Color Temperatures

as red, blue, or yellow. Thus one speaks of a color *with* a red hue, or a color that *has* a red hue. Second, *hue* may refer to a color that is pure in the sense of not having been mixed or adulterated with other colorants that would reduce its spectral reflectance and thereby lessen its impact of expression. Technically, when a hue or pure color is mixed with black, white, grays or other colors that lessen its purity, it is no longer considered a hue but instead is a member of a family of colors that share a hue. All colorant hues used directly from the manufacturer's tubes, jars, and/or bottles, are considered pure unless labeled otherwise. Ultramarine blue, permanent green, and the cadmium hues are all good examples of pure colorants. The modulated colors that are now appearing on the market are mixtures of a hue plus white (a tint) or a hue plus black (a shade) or even a gray of equal lightness or darkness to the original hue. Because these colors are not pure, they do not carry the same impact of expression as does a hue.

A traditional approach to understanding hue and hue relationships is the visible light spectrum curved into a circle and then approximated in pigment. On such a color wheel or (more accurately) *hue circle*, complementary hues lie opposite one another. When the hue circle is made with the light spectrum and kept as light, the complements additively mix to form white light. But when the hue circle is translated into pigment, the resultant mix is subtractive and produces either a dull brown or a black, depending on the hue circle employed.

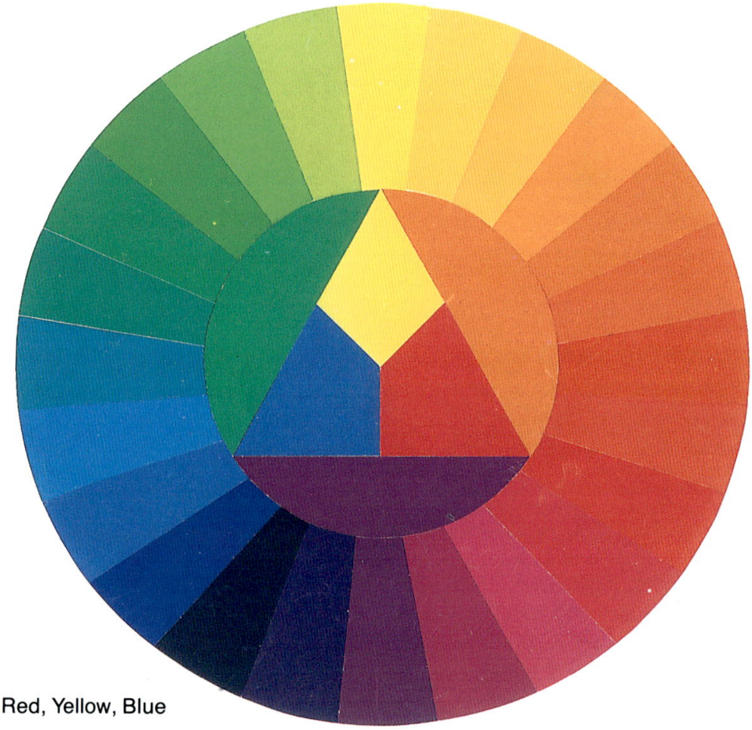

Figure 2-4 Hue Circle of the Red, Yellow, Blue (RYB) System

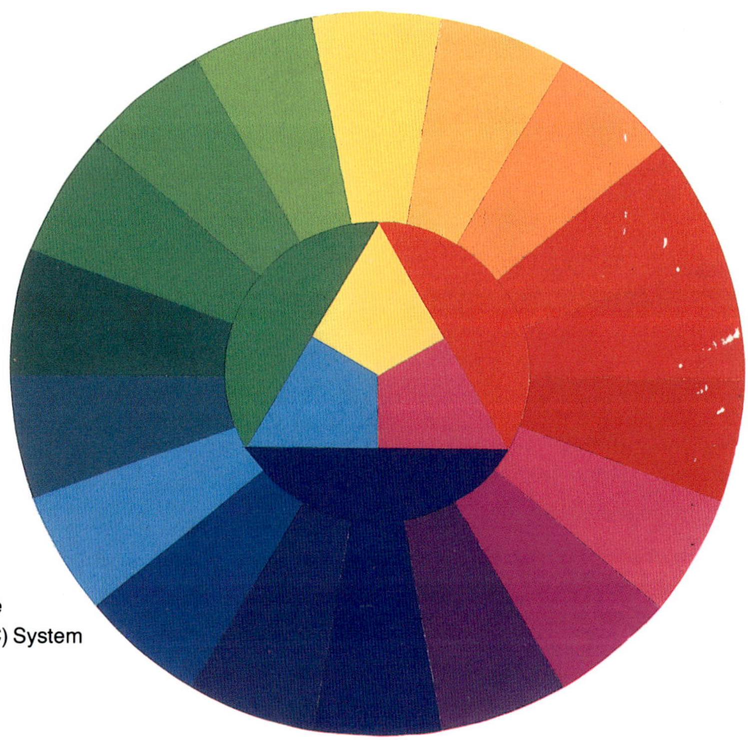

Figure 2-6 Hue Circle of the Magenta, Yellow, Cyan (MYC) System

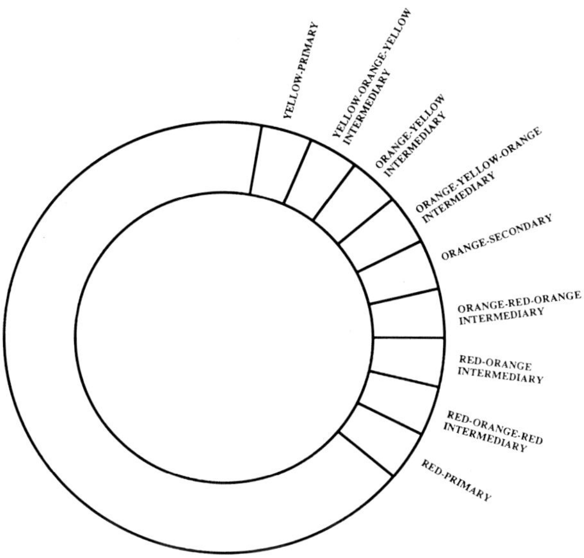

Figure 2-5 Primary Arc of Yellow to Red

COLORANT HUE CIRCLES

Two colorant hue circle systems are in use today. The first of these uses red (R), yellow (Y), and blue (B) as its primary hues (hues that cannot be mixed from other hues) and may be called the RYB system. The secondary hues of the RYB system are simple mixtures of the two primary hues that lie on either side of each secondary on the circle (figure 2-4); thus, yellow + red = orange, red + blue = violet, and yellow + blue = green. The secondary hues are *not* composed of equal mixtures of their primaries, because the tinctorial power—that is, the ability of one hue or color to change the character of another hue or color—is not the same for each primary. For example, a great deal more yellow is needed to shift a blue toward green than the amount of blue required to shift a yellow toward green. Hence the blue has much greater tinctorial power than the yellow. In general, darker colors tend to have greater tinctorial power than lighter colors (see Chapter 5). The hues that lie between primary and secondary hues are called *intermediaries* or *intermediary hues*. The number of intermediaries depends on the total number of hues in a given hue circle (figure 2-5).

The second hue circle system also contains primaries, secondaries, and intermediaries, but the hues are a *direct translation* of the visible spectrum into pigment. For this reason it may be called the MYC system, because the primaries in it are magenta, yellow, and cyan (figure 2-6). The MYC system has a decided advantage over the RYB system in the area of color mixing, since an interesting inverted image relationship exists between the light hue circle and the colorant hue circle. If the light secondaries are translated into pigment, true subtractive mixing takes place, and the resulting mix of these hues is black. Therefore, the MYC system represents a more accurate hue circle for true complements. In essence, it is the light hue circle transposed to pigment and then reversed so that the primary/secondary relationship is now magenta/green, cyan/red-orange, and yellow/blue-violet. For color mixing, the MYC hue circle gives accurate and consistent results and is also consistent with other color phenomena in perception (see Chapter 4). And while the relationships and color approximations found in the RYB system are by no means invalid, the mixing results in that system are somewhat unpredictable.

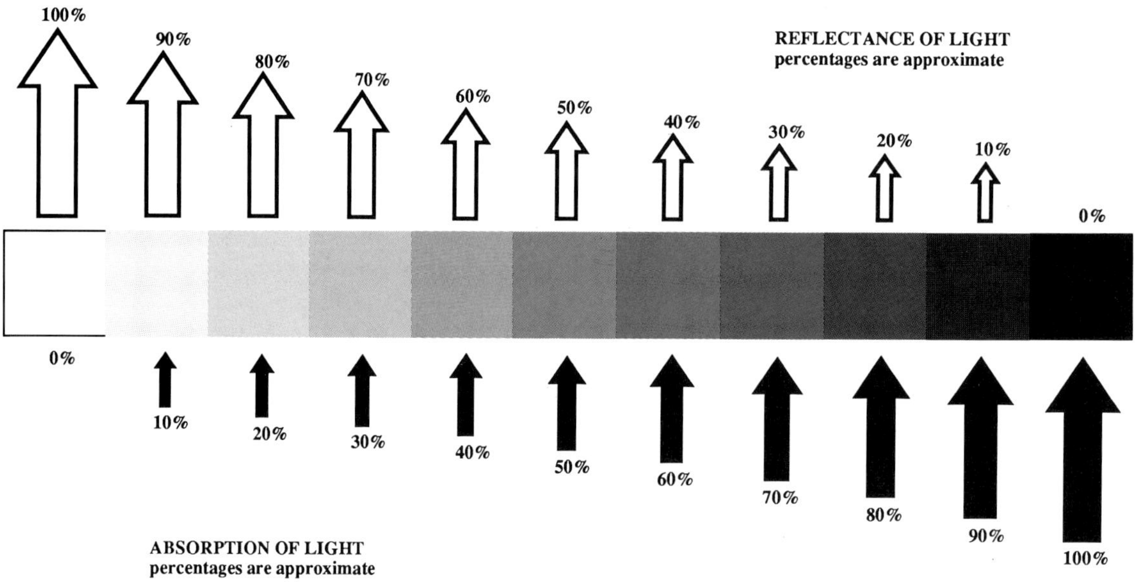

Figure 2-7 Reflectance (upper row of arrows) and Absorption (lower row of arrows) of Light

Figures 2-4 and 2-6 illustrate two hue circles. The first is a 24-hue circle based on the RYB system. The second, an 18-hue circle, is based on the MYC or light hue system. The relationships between families of hues are easily understood when the families are compared. The discrepancy in numbers of hues per system, however, is arbitrary and can be tailored by the individual artist to the practical purposes at hand.

The advantages of making hue circles for reference tools in the studio are many. A hue circle can provide a visualization of all intermediary hues (within visual limits) possible between a particular pair of primary and secondary hues. Like perfect pitch in music, perfect color recall is a rare phenomenon; the hue circle becomes a memory peg for maintaining consistent color systems in designing. Another sound argument for using hue circles for reference is to ensure the accurate use of complementary hues. Many beautiful complementary combinations are found in compound hues such as blue-green (BG) to orange-red (OR) or violet-red-violet (VRV) to yellow-green-yellow (YGY)—and again these are very difficult to keep in one's memory. (This example uses the RYB system; the complements in the MYC system would be slightly different.)

Hues that lie near or next to other hues on any hue circle are called *analogs* or *analogous hues*.

Value

By definition, *value* is a color's percentage of totally reflected or absorbed light. Here, *totality* means that reflection is *not* selective or

a

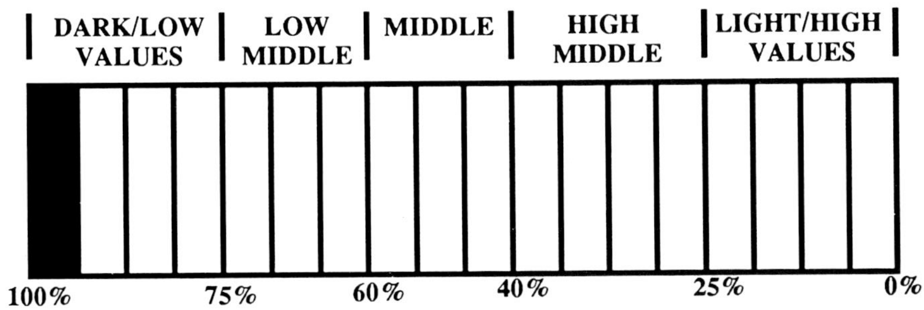

b

Figure 2-8 Gray or Value Scale: (a) The scale itself; (b) Percentages of light absorption.

chromatic, but nonselective or achromatic. White is seen when all wavelengths of visible light hitting a surface are reflected. No specific color—that is, no selective spectral reflection—is present. Black, on the other hand, reflects a negligible number of wavelengths, and we generalize by saying that black reflects no visible light. Depending on how much black is mixed with white (the stronger tinctorial pigment is mixed into the weaker for better mixing control), fewer and fewer wavelengths of light will be reflected and more and more wavelengths will be absorbed, producing darker and darker grays or values.

Many artists, designers, printers, and other people working in the commercial visual arts speak of values in terms of percentage of absorption rather than in terms of reflectance; photographers are an exception and most often refer to reflectance, because of the types of equipment used. When speaking of absorption, the numbers are reversed. White is 0 percent absorption; black is 100 percent. A 50 percent value is a gray that falls approximately midway between black and white. Values can be described quickly with a good deal of accuracy just by referring to a percentage. Thus, 10 percent is a light value and 80 percent is a dark value (figure 2-7).

A useful tool for controlling value and thereby controlling color is a graded series of values that range from black to white; it is known variously as a value scale, a gray scale, or an achromatic scale (figure 2-8). The scale

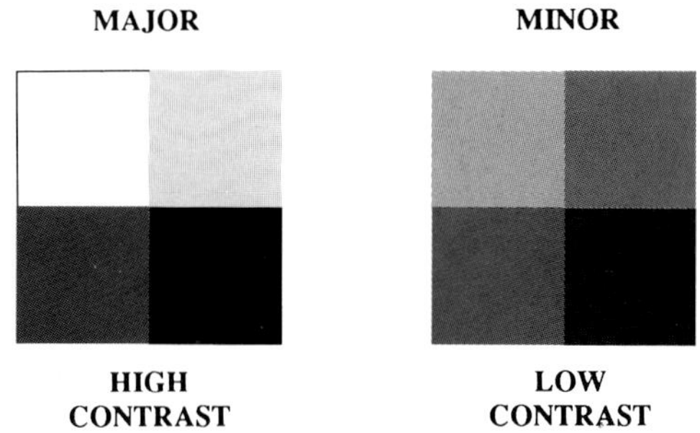

Figure 2-9 Relative Contrast Between Major and Minor Keys

is roughly divided into five sections or areas that, in terms of light and dark, describe a feeling or mood: high or light, 0 to 25 percent; high middle, 25 to 40 percent; middle, 40 to 60 percent; low middle, 60 to 75 percent; low or dark, 75 to 100 percent (figure 2-8). The absorption percentages that accompany the mood descriptions are only approximations. They can become confusing when a value is described as light or high and then has an accompanying percentage description of 10 percent. For this reason it may be helpful when starting out to relate the value scale to a piano keyboard, keeping the black to the left (or at the bottom, if one is reading the scale vertically). The low notes of a keyboard are on the left, as are the low or dark values (or they are down and low, as compared to up or high, when seen vertically). This separates the verbal description from the percentages of absorption and becomes easier to recall.

Although value is only one of the four properties inherent in every color, it may be used independently. Therefore, a design may first be executed in value before it is translated into color (see Chapter 3)—an excellent habit to develop.

VALUE KEYS

Seven different organizations of values may be used to evoke specific emotional responses in the viewer. These are called *value keys*. The value key of a work describes the organization and relationship between specific values, which in turn are read subliminally by the viewer as a translation of light or light level on a two-dimensional plane. We respond to light level or to our sense of lightness and/or darkness before we respond visually to hue and/or color. Our response to light is immediate, and it is both physical and emotional. We each have a preference for a quality of light, a time of day with which we feel most comfortable. We react so universally to light levels that values may be orchestrated to obtain predetermined responses. This can be

Figure 2-10 Distribution of Values in the Major Keys: (a) High major; (b) Middle major; (c) Low major.

a

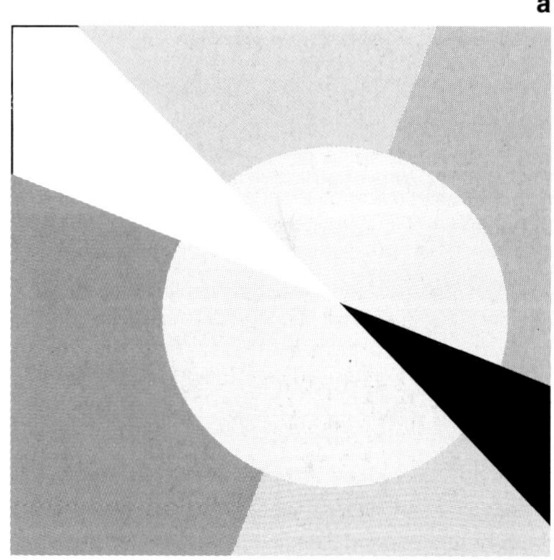

a very useful tool in controlling color! Understanding and using value keys does not exclude using other value organizations that do not fall into a specific key category. Value keys serve only to evoke specific moods.

The seven value keys fall into two large categories, *major* and *minor*, and are not unlike those of music. Major tonalities in music tend to be direct, outgoing, and assertive, with greater tonal distances or contrast between intervals. Minor tonalities are closer in interval relationships or have less contrast between intervals, and they give a more subdued, quiet, or perhaps sad feeling (figure 2-9).

The value keys in the visual arts work in a similar way. The major keys all show contrast; they all contain both black and white, with changes in the proportion, quantity, or dominance of the values used. The major keys are divided into three groups—high major, middle major, and low major—each of which is named for the dominant group of values used. The high major key has a dominance of high or light values, which include white and values perceived as white that also contain a small amount of black (figure 2-10a). This key tends to give a happy feeling, an almost luminous and vivacious sense; it is hard to be despondent at high noon on a sunny day. The middle major key is dominated by middle values and contains roughly equal amounts of white and black (figure 2-10b). Many visual artists tend naturally to use the middle major. This key gives a feeling of great stability, directness, and strength. It possesses a strong, well-balanced, posteresque distribution of values. The third major key is the low major. This key is theatrical—sometimes mysterious and somber, but always dramatic. The dominance falls into the low or dark value range, which

b

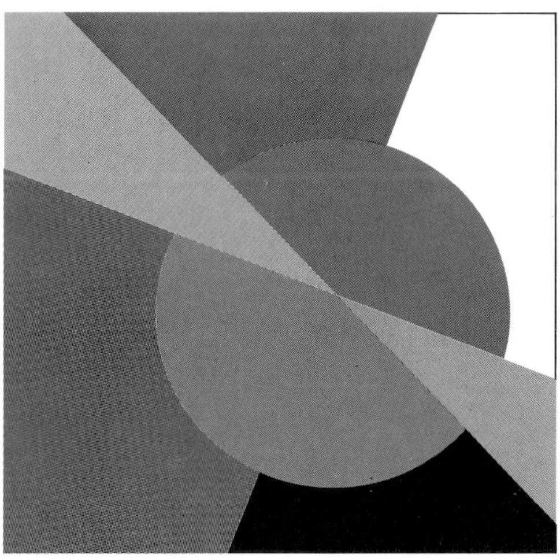

c

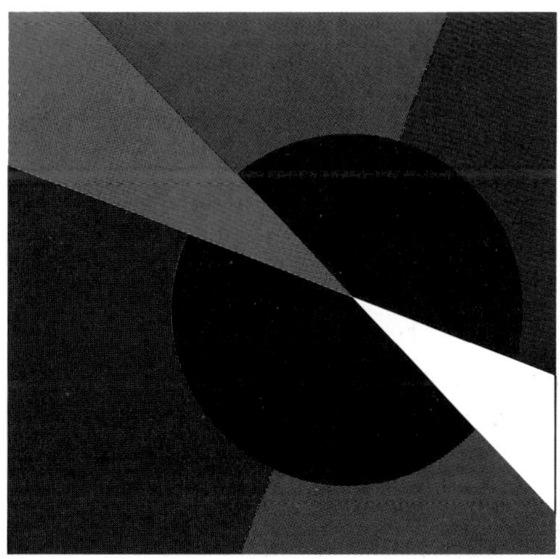

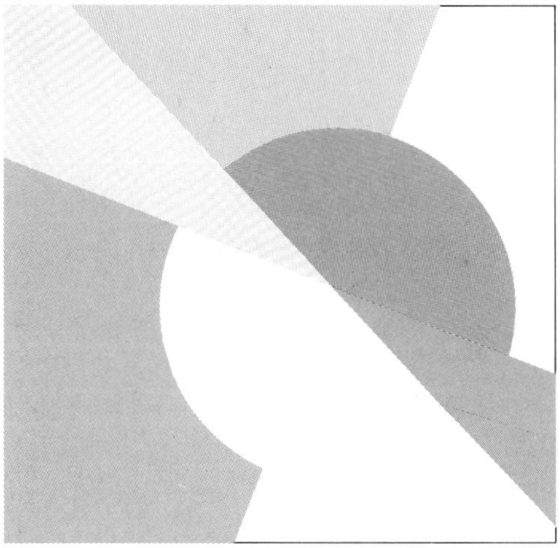
a

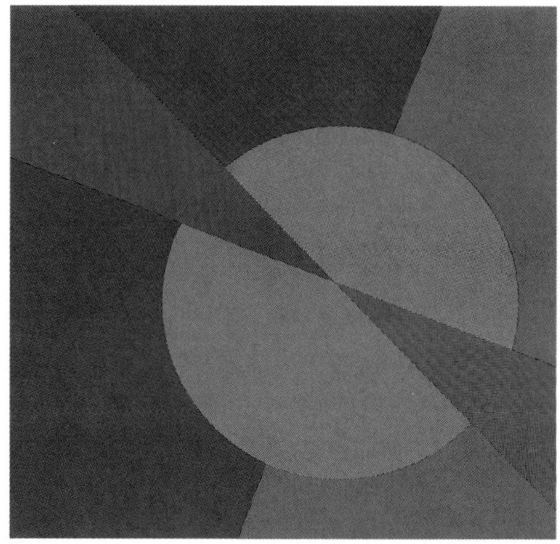
b

Figure 2-11 Distribution of Values in the Minor Keys: (a) High minor; (b) Middle minor; (c) Low minor; (d) Extended middle minor.

includes black and values perceived as black that also contain a small amount of very light or white value (figure 2-10c).

The principal difference between the major and minor keys involves contrast. The minor keys do *not* include the entire value scale; instead, the keys consist of groups of closely related values within a limited range. The four minor keys are: high minor, middle minor, low minor, and extended middle minor. The high minor consists entirely of values from the high or light end of the value scale—0 to 25 percent, approximately. This key evokes feelings of serenity and peace characterized by great delicacy (figure 2-11a). The middle minor takes values from the midrange of the value scale, 40 to 60 percent. These middle values also convey a sense of quiet atmosphere, but the feeling of light is more subdued, dense yet strong. Because the light is neither high nor low, the mood is less well defined; nonetheless, it is calm and dreamlike (figure 2-11b). The low minor, which takes its values from the low or dark end of the value scale, has been called depressed, gloomy, sinister, introspective, and funereal. The value percentages here range from approximately 75 to 100 percent (figure 2-11c). The extended middle minor contains values from 25 to 75 percent. As its name implies, it extends the range of the middle minor to produce an organization of values that show slightly more contrast. The feeling of light level is ambiguous. By definition, it is neither major nor minor; it loses some of the serenity of the middle minor without developing the high contrast and visual stability of the middle major. The light level suggests a surreal or fantasy mood (figure 2-11d).

Color design problems often originate from value designs that are confusing or lack struc-

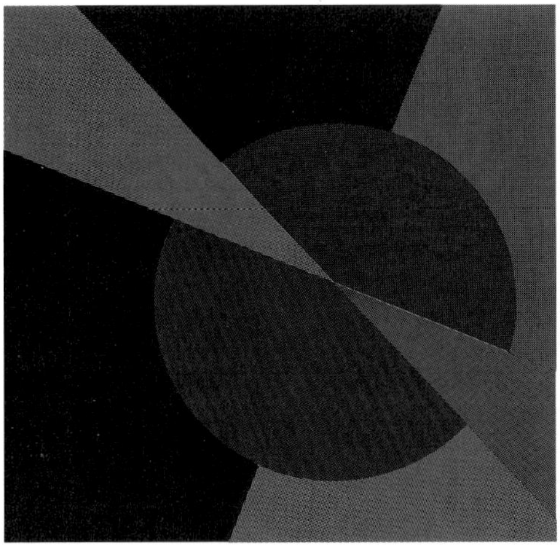

c

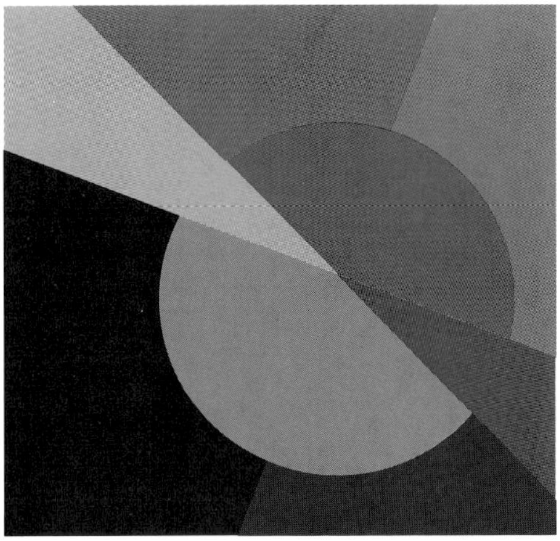

d

ture. Often the artist tries to fix hue relationships before checking the value relationships. It is advisable to make value roughs, especially when visual thinking is unclear.

Intensity

There are probably more synonyms in the color literature describing the intensity of a color than any other characteristic. As misleading as some of them may be, they are all defined as the relative *degree of purity* of a reflected color. The terms in use are *intensity, purity, saturation, strength, density, chroma,* and *brightness/dullness.* Often the terms *lightness* and *brightness* are interchanged, which can make color description even more confusing. When used correctly, *lightness* refers to value, and *brightness* refers to purity or how much hue a color contains. Pink, for example, is a light value of red but contains little red in comparison to the hue; therefore, the brightness or intensity is low. It has a high feeling of light, but a low feeling of color.

The intensity of a hue or color may be lowered in five ways, either as single manipulations or in combination: by tinting, by shading, by toning, by complementary mixing, and by adding a third primary in any proportion. A *tint* is a combination of a hue or color and white, in any proportion. A *shade* is a combination of a hue or color and black, in any proportion. Both tints and shades, when used in design as juxtaposed shapes to one or more areas of the original hue, create a strong sense of space within the design (figure 2-12). The more intense the color, the more it appears to come forward or advance. This illustrates the phrase *relative degree of purity* quite clearly. The tints and shades look more intense if the hue is

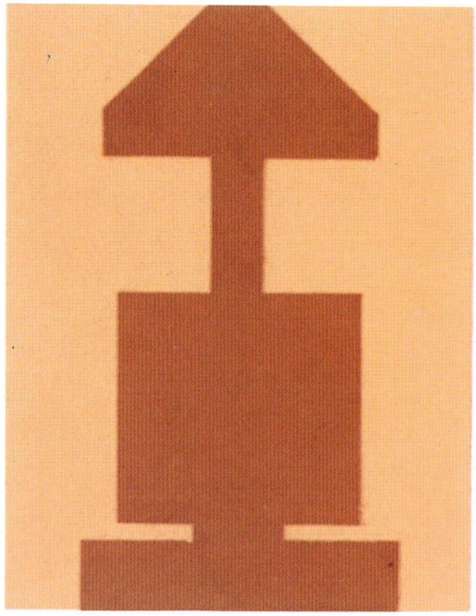
a

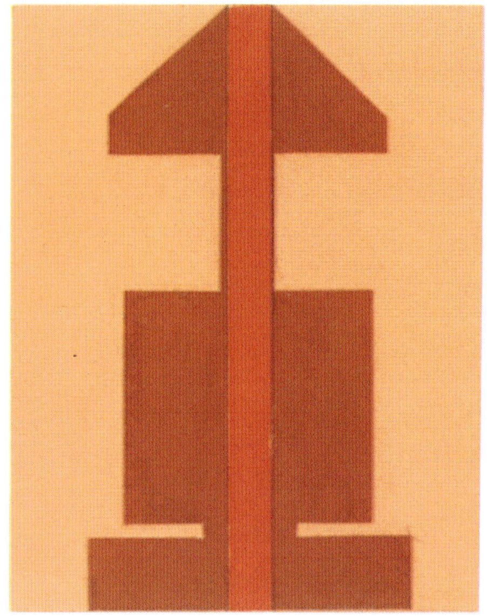
b

Figure 2-12 Sense of Space Created by Juxtapositions of Tint, Shade, and Hue: (a) Tint and shade without hue; (b) Tint and shade with hue.

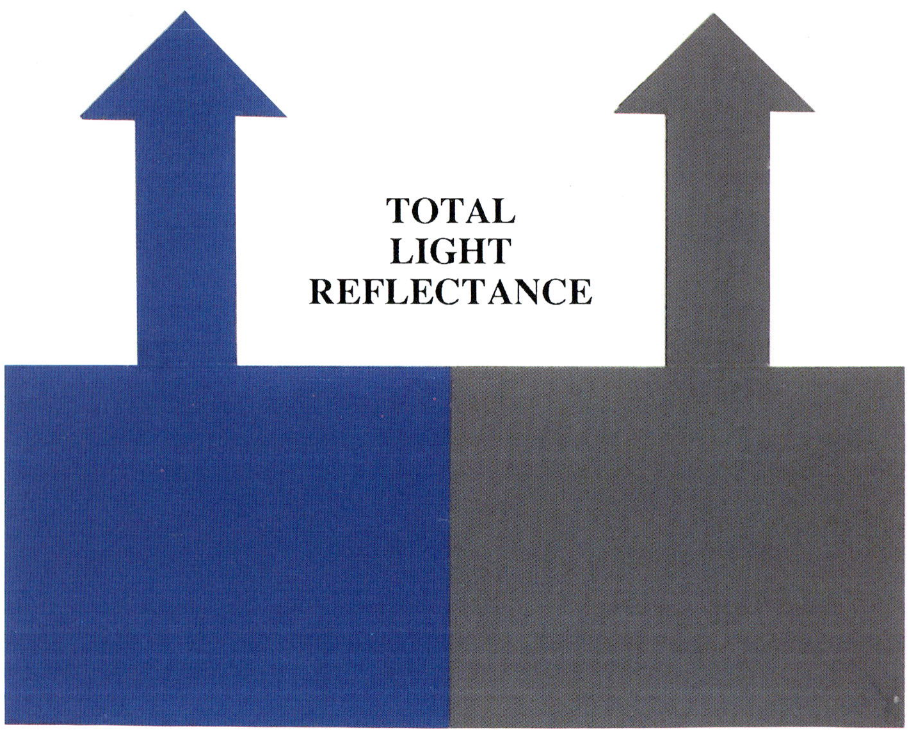

Figure 2-13 Color and Its Relative Value

absent; when the hue is present, the tints and shades appear to lose some intensity.

A *tone* is a hue or color in combination with a gray of the same *relative value* (see Chapter 3). The relative value of a hue or color is the particular gray that matches the hue or color in total light reflectance/absorption (figure 2-13).

The fourth and fifth methods of lowering intensity are related. The fourth approach is to add the complement to a hue or color. This method, called *direct complementary mixing*, is particularly useful for slightly lowering a hue's intensity without changing its essential character (figure 2-14). The fifth method, called *indirect complementary mixing*, produces more varied results (see Chapter 5), because there are more possibilities. For example, when yellow and red are mixed in any arbitrary amount, an orange is produced that changes the hue of the yellow to a yellow-orange but does not lower the intensity of the yellow. Similarly, adding blue to a yellow produces a green (depending on the quantity of blue added), again without lowering the intensity of the yellow. If, however, red with a small amount of blue in it—that is RVR (red-violet-

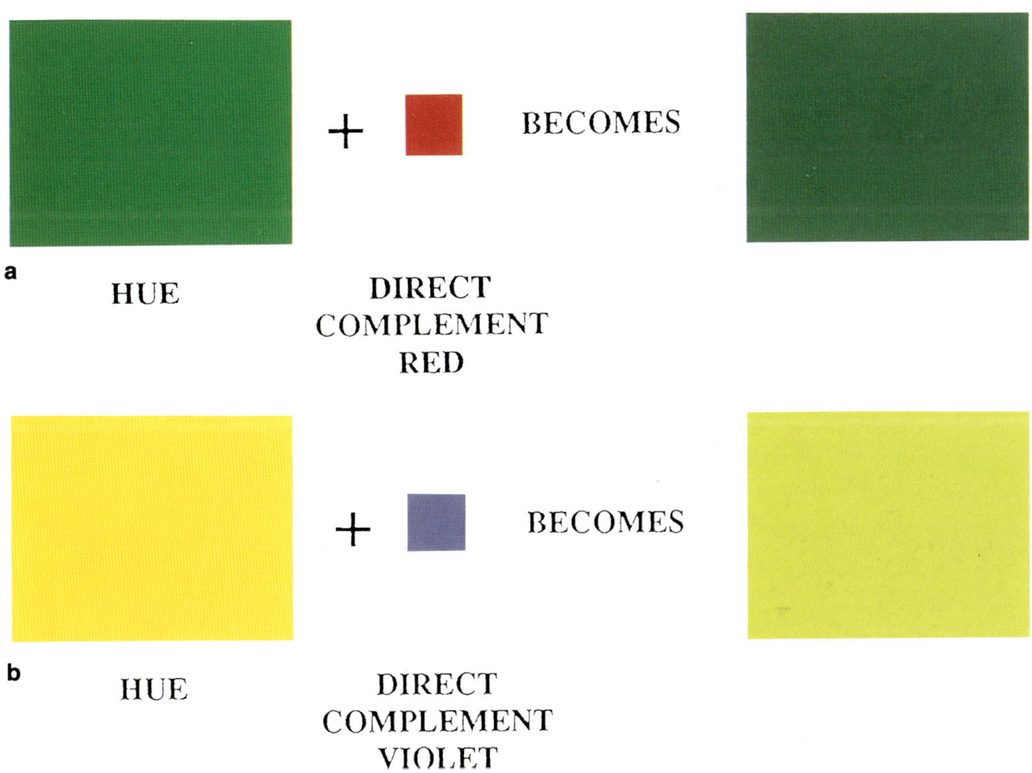

Figure 2-14 Direct Complementary Mixing: (a) Hue + direct complement red; (b) Hue + direct complement violet.

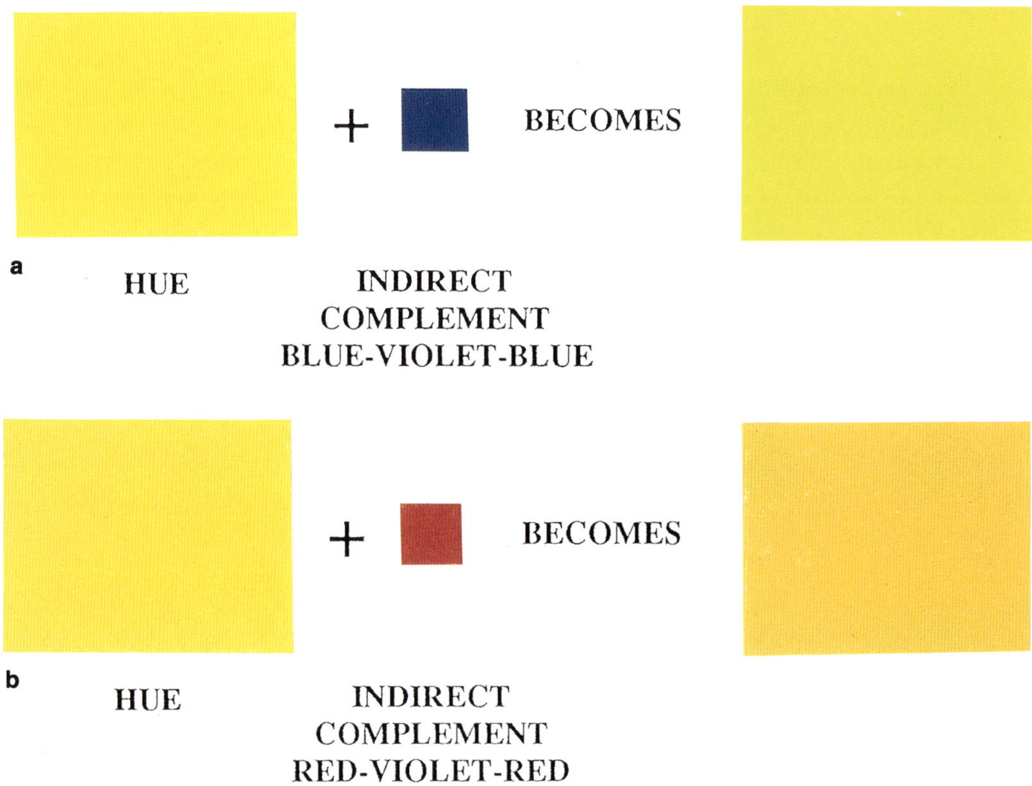

Figure 2-15 Indirect Complementary Mixing: (a) Hue + indirect complement red-violet-red; (b) Hue + indirect complement blue-violet-blue.

red) (figure 2-15)—were added to the yellow, the intensity of the original yellow would be lowered and a new, less intense color produced. Conversely, if a blue with a small amount of red in it (BVB) were mixed with the yellow, the same thing would occur. When all three primary hues of either hue system are added together in any proportion, the intensity of the original hue or color is lowered. Very beautiful colors can be made in this way. Chapter 5 illustrates these last two methods of lowering intensity more fully.

Temperature

The *temperature* of a reflected color or hue is defined as its relative degree of warmth or coolness; this quality affects us psychologically and to some extent physically. The warm colors are red, orange, and yellow, while the cool ones are blue, green, and violet. Color temperature can easily be visualized with the help of a hue circle (figure 2-16). The three 120-degree arcs running from yellow to red (YR), red to blue (RB), an blue to yellow (BY) may be called primary arcs. The YR arc

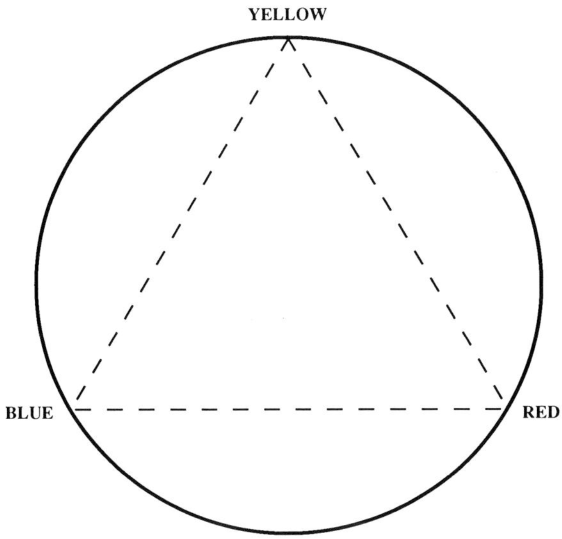

Figure 2-16 The Three Primary Arcs

includes only hues that are made up of yellow and red; therefore, only the hues that fall within this arc are totally warm, and the warmest or most polarized hue is orange. There is absolutely no blue within this arc. There is no yellow in the RB arc, just as there is no red in the BY arc. Blue is the hue most polarized with orange to show coolness. Thus, besides being complementary hues, blue and orange demonstrate the extremes of color temperature (figure 2-17). Compound hues such as YGY and RVR have characteristics of both warm and cool colors. As a result, they are called *temperate* hues or colors. Their temperature characteristics change, depending on what hues or colors are used around them.

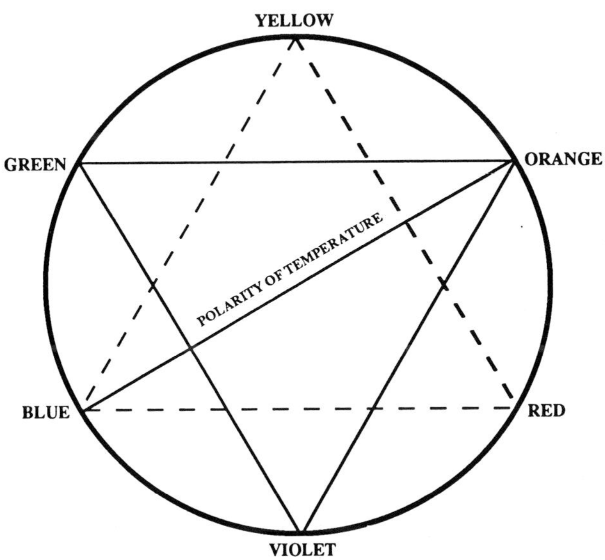

Figure 2-17 The Three Secondary Arcs, Showing Polarity of Temperature

3 COLOR SYNCHRONICITY

Understanding the color properties in Chapter 2 is essential for the next step of study, which involves combining these color properties so that they may be used with aesthetic judgment and control. In order to use these properties effectively and productively, it is necessary to understand them in relation to one another.

Hue and Value

From our primitive origins, we have been fascinated and controlled by the constant change of light in our environment. Indeed, we may react to changes in light and dark (value) before we react to color (hue). If this is so, then the importance to the artist/designer of understanding value and value keys cannot be overemphasized. But putting a visual image into values that produce a desired emotional expression is just the beginning. The artist/designer must then be able to translate the value design into the appropriate colors, to keep the initial light/dark feeling as well as to exploit color expressiveness.

Because color and hue exist between the limits of light (white) and dark (black), every color and/or hue has its counterpart in a value that reflects or absorbs the same amount of light. The artist/designer must know how to translate color and hue into value and vice versa.

The simplest method of learning to translate color into value is to use the value scale described in Chapter 2. It is possible to buy gray papers at an art supply store or to make a value scale by mixing black and white paint (see Chapter 5). After the scale is complete, an ordinary hole puncher may be used to put holes in each step of the scale—either on one or both sides (figure 3-1). One side may be used as a control for a variety of colors, and

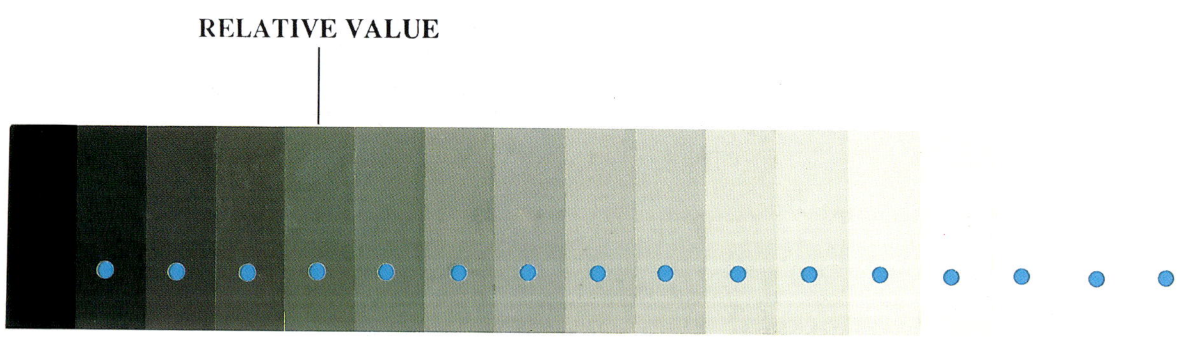

Figure 3-1 Value Scale for Determining the Relative Value of a Color

the other set of holes may be left open for determining value/color (hue) relationships. Include at least 15 steps in the scale, and proceed by using the method of mixing described in Chapter 5.

Every color/hue has a *relative value*—a corresponding gray that matches the lightness or darkness or that color/hue. The most efficient match is achieved if a conscious effort is made to squint at the color that is visible through the hole. Squinting reduces the amount of light entering the eye and allows the photoreceptors at the back of the eye (called the *rods*) to increase their activity. Two kinds of photoreceptors in the eye are sensitive to light and color: the rods are sensitive in low light and to values; and the cones are sensitive to color, high light, and detail. Since squinting reduces the amount of light entering the eye, it increases the activity of the rods and decreases the activity of the cones (to a degree), thereby making it easier to match a color/hue to a value accurately.

Bright or very intense light is to be avoided when matching hue to value, because in this case one cannot squint hard enough to lower the light level coming into the eye. Very low light is also undesirable, because at low light levels it becomes difficult to distinguish between small shifts in value and color. The best light is provided by a full-spectrum lamp or medium-level daylight, where squinting renders a color or hue in the best relationship to a value.

It is important to use a small area of color within a larger area of value. Even if the match is done outside the context of a value scale, a small piece of color should be placed on a larger piece of value to test it (figure 3-2). If the swatches are painted, wait until each is thoroughly dry before making a determination. If a small sample of value is placed on a color or hue the results are unlikely to be accurate, because simultaneous contrast (see Chapter 4) will create a color shift in the value.

Reds and oranges are the most difficult to

Figure 3-2 Yellow and Its Relative Value

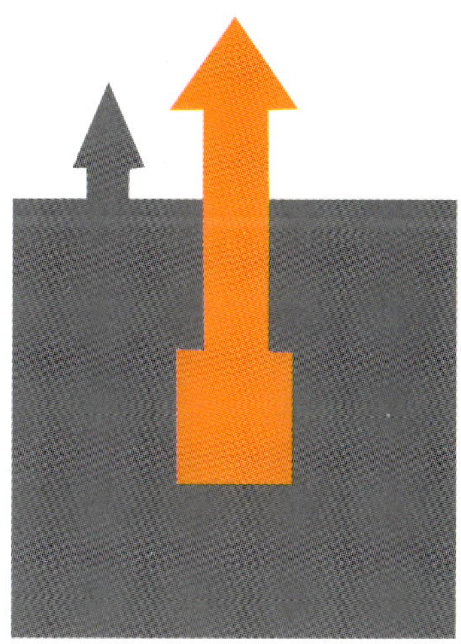

Figure 3-3 Orange and Its Relative Value

place on the value scale. The relative values of these colors are usually darker than one would expect. Red and orange wavelengths of light appear to advance toward the viewer when reflected from a surface, producing misleading results (figure 3-3). Practice increases one's ability quickly, however, and soon the concept of relative value becomes an integral part of overall color control.

Hue and Intensity

Many different words in the lexicon of color are used to describe color properties and attributes. One of the most confusing is the word *tone*. In some visual disciplines—printing and photography, in particular—the word *tone* refers to value. This may have originated in the printing field, where a visual image that has a full range of values from black to white (such as paintings, photographs, and drawings) is known as continuous-tone copy, and where any group of values representing the values of the original continuous-tone copy is known as a halftone because of the method of reproduction. Once again, each specialized field uses its own specific terminology, and this can be confusing to the beginner. Regrettably a standardized vocabulary is not the norm for all visual art.

As defined in the aesthetic use of color, *tone* and *tonality* mean two different things. *Tone* refers to a quality change in the intensity or purity of a hue or color, but rarely is the precise definition used: a color achieved by mixing a color or hue with its relative value so that *only* the intensity (and not the value) is changed. *Tonality*, on the other hand, refers to the overall feeling that a value key evokes—somberness, happiness, tranquility, or the like. The mood of an image is synonymous with its tonality. In popular usage, *tone* is broadly employed to indicate any color or color change. This is very misleading and says nothing of any substance about the color itself or about changes in that color.

Value and Intensity

Controlling color presupposes that essential terms are completely understood—both intellectually and emotionally—and that the visual application is accurate. The terms *value and intensity* are not difficult in themselves, but often they are misinterpreted visually. The following scales, as well as the discussion in Chapter 2, should dispel any confusion.

The first scale represents tinting a hue (figure 3-4). As the color grows less intense, the value gets lighter, until the last step (which is a white) shows 0 percent color. The scale starts with a 100 percent color or hue; then, as the color is more and more diluted with white, its intensity gets lower and lower and its value gets higher and higher. The second scale represents shading a hue (figure 3-5). This time, black is added to the hue in successive steps. Again, the hue starts out 100 percent pure, and as each color is shaded the color content is lowered until there is no color left; thus, again the final step is a value of 0 percent color. The intensity has gone down, and so has the value.

The third scale represents toning a hue (figure 3-6). The relative value of the hue was mixed from black and white and has 0 percent

Figure 3-4 Tint Scale: Value increases and intensity decreases

Figure 3-5 Shade Scale: Value decreases and intensity decreases

Figure 3-6 Tone Scale: Value stays the same and intensity decreases

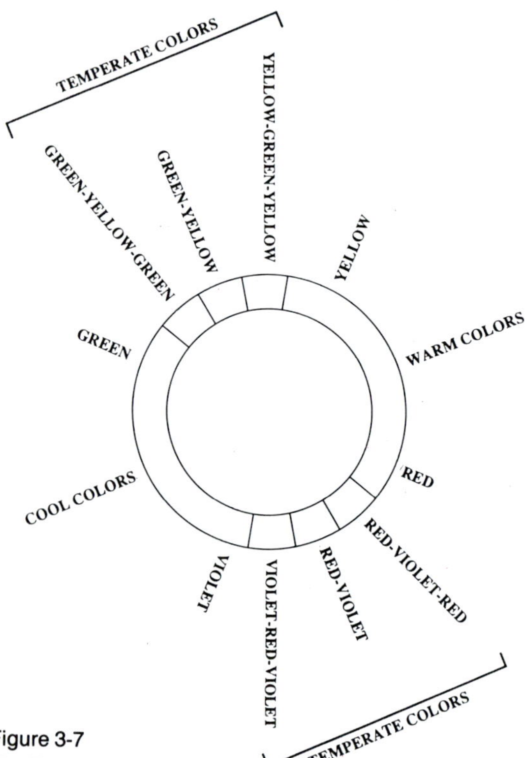

Figure 3-7
The Temperate Colors

color content. In this scale, although the intensity has been lowered from 100 percent to 0 percent, the value of the scale has remained constant.

Hue and Temperature

The temperature of a color is defined as being warm (red, orange, and yellow), cool (blue, violet, and green), or temperate (red-violets and yellow-greens) (figure 3-7).

When a paint pigment is knifed or brushed out straight from the tube or jar, the paint's opaque or solid color effect is called its *body color*. Each pigment has not only a body color but a characteristic *undertone*. The undertone of a pigment color or hue is the color effect produced when that pigment is tinted, diluted

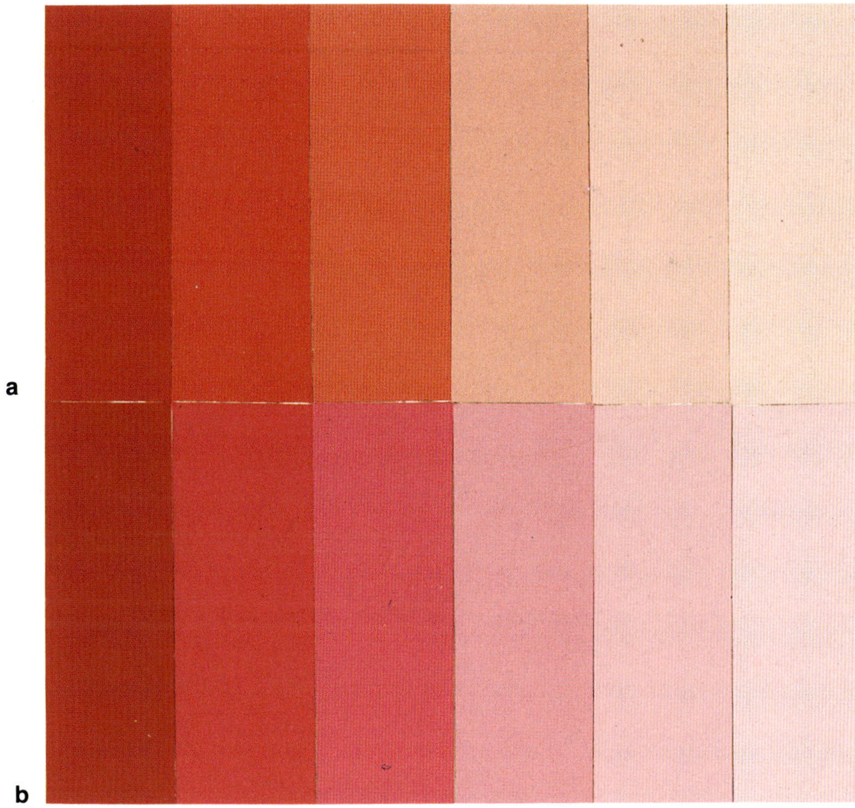

Figure 3-8 Undertones of Two Reds: (a) Red with an undertone of yellow; (b) Red with an undertone of blue.

with its solvent (such as water in acrylic or watercolor paint), or made into a transparent film as in a glaze (see Chapter 5).

Undertones are most easily seen when two hues of the same family are compared. For example, two reds showing similar body color may tint out very differently (figure 3-8); here, one red (a) shows a yellow or orange quality, and the other (b) a bluer quality. Undertones fall into the primary categories of red, yellow, and blue, and are a vital part of controlling color. Color expression can be weakened or inhibited by using a color with an undertone that either works against the design or is incompatible in a mixture.

Undertones mark temperature shifts rather than actual hue shifts, and they can subtly convey the illusion of advancing and/or receding planes within an area of analogous color—warm undertones advancing, and cool undertones receding (figure 3-9).

Hue, Value, Intensity, and Temperature

To gain the greatest control over aesthetic color expression, an artist/designer must consider the four color properties collectively, with each color a function of those collective properties. Of course, learning the identity of each as a separate entity is essential, but with

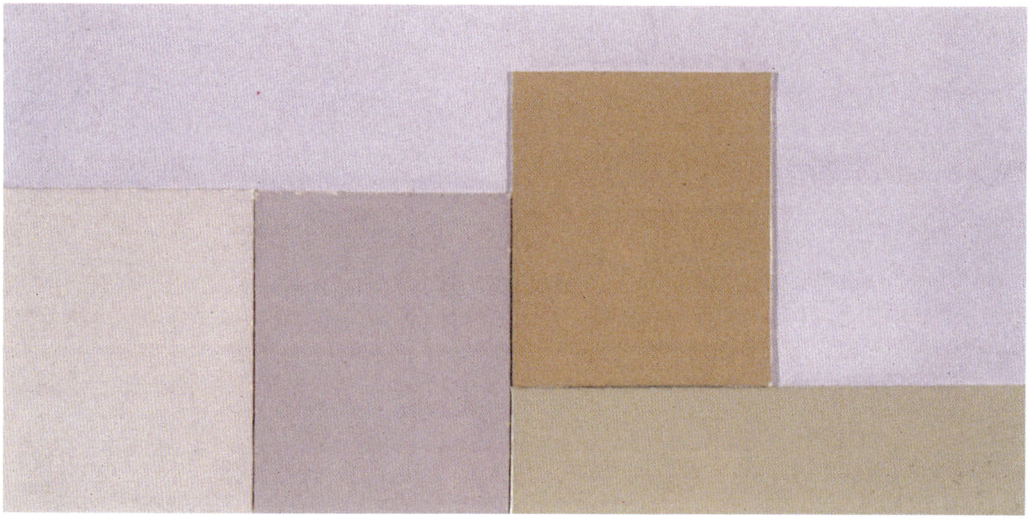

Figure 3-9 Temperature Shifts in Color, Demonstrating Advancing and Receding Planes in Space

the foundation in place and as awareness and familiarity increase, it will no longer be possible to think of one property without thinking of the others.

Many artists and designers, when beginning an in-depth study of color, assume that most color problems are simply a matter of changing a hue or a color. But in reality most color problems involve handling values and dealing with spatial effects by using altered temperatures or intensities. Although the choice of hue and color is vital, it does not stand alone and indeed may not even stand first in consideration.

One color is always relative to another; no color may be described as a permanent, unchanging reality, because as soon as it is surrounded by another color its character changes. A series of green tones is a good example of the deceptive nature of color and our senses. Controlling, by choice, as many variables as possible will simplify the exercise. In this case hue, value, and temperature are all controlled, and the only variable is intensity (figure 3-10). If step 1 is omitted, the second tone looks quite intense. If steps 1, 2, 3, and 4 are all omitted, the fifth tone looks a good deal more intense then the succeeding ones, and so on. The tone that has the most intensity depends on relativity and comparison.

Controlling color ultimately becomes a continuing exercise in the orchestration and manipulation of its properties, and such an exercise is only possible by means of comparisons and contrasts.

Color Harmony

The phrase *color harmony* is another confusing term often connected with a variety of meanings.

Harmony, a principle of design, usually refers to the use of similar design elements—similar lines, shapes, textures, and so on (figure 3-11). Color and value (the one color property that may exist independent of the others) are also design elements; thus, *color harmony* in the design sense means colors and/or values that are analogs or are related by some similarity (figure 3-12).

However, another definition of *color harmony* is an outgrowth of color theory and utilizes the concept of color completeness, or complementarity. This concept of color harmony strives for balance in color design and relates to a hue's reflectance.

In 1810, assigning an arbitrary number of 10 to white and 0 to black, the German poet and color theorist Johann Wolfgang von Goethe observed that two qualities determine the impact of a hue in color expression. The

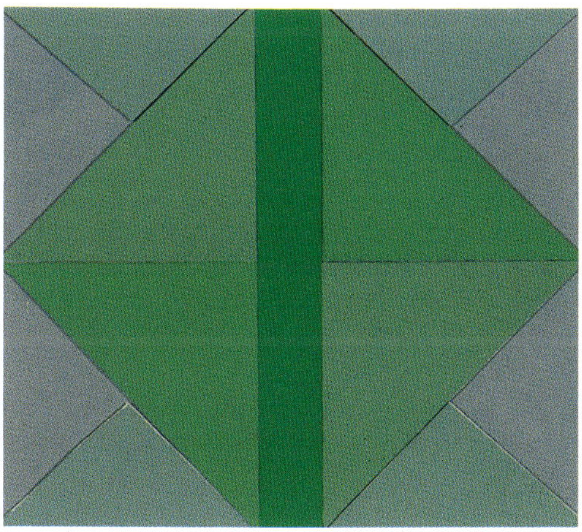

Figure 3-10 Intensity Changes, Producing a Sense of Space

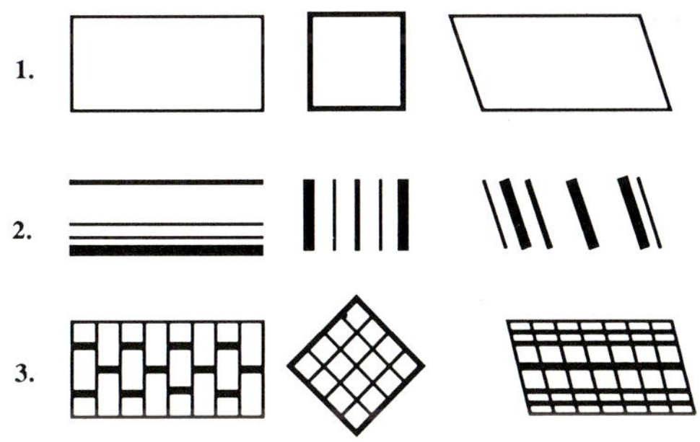

Figure 3-11 Harmonious Shapes (1), Lines (2), and Patterns (3)

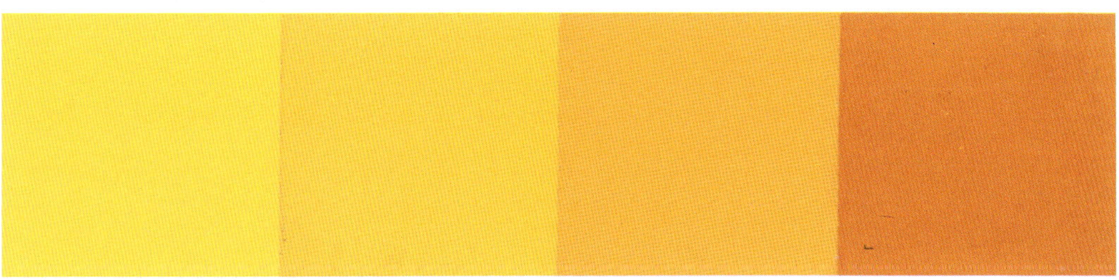

Figure 3-12 Analogous Hues

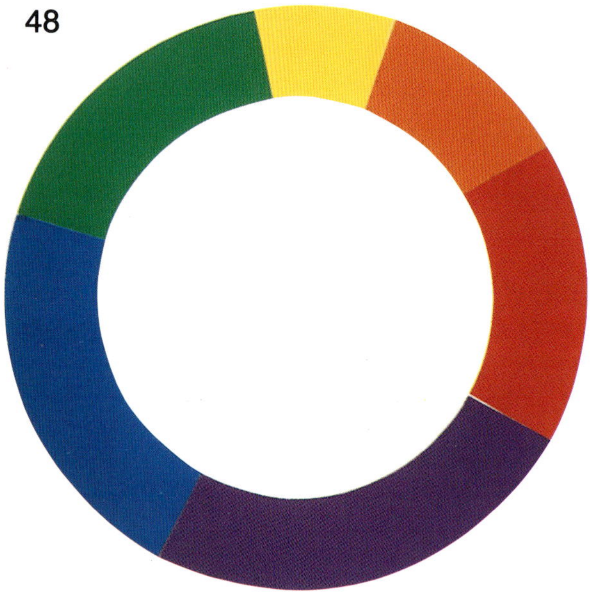

Figure 3-13 Circle of Primary and Secondary Hues in Harmonious Proportion

first is its value, and the second is the proportion or quantity of the hue used in the design. Goethe, basing his results on the value scale he devised from 10 to 0 (no color has a relative value of white or black), determined the following scale values: yellow = 9, orange = 8, red = 6, green = 6, blue = 4, and violet = 3. Comparing complements, and expressing the relationship of each by a ratio, we find the following:

yellow : violet = 9:3, or 3:1
orange:blue = 8:4, or 2:1
red:green = 6:6, or 1:1

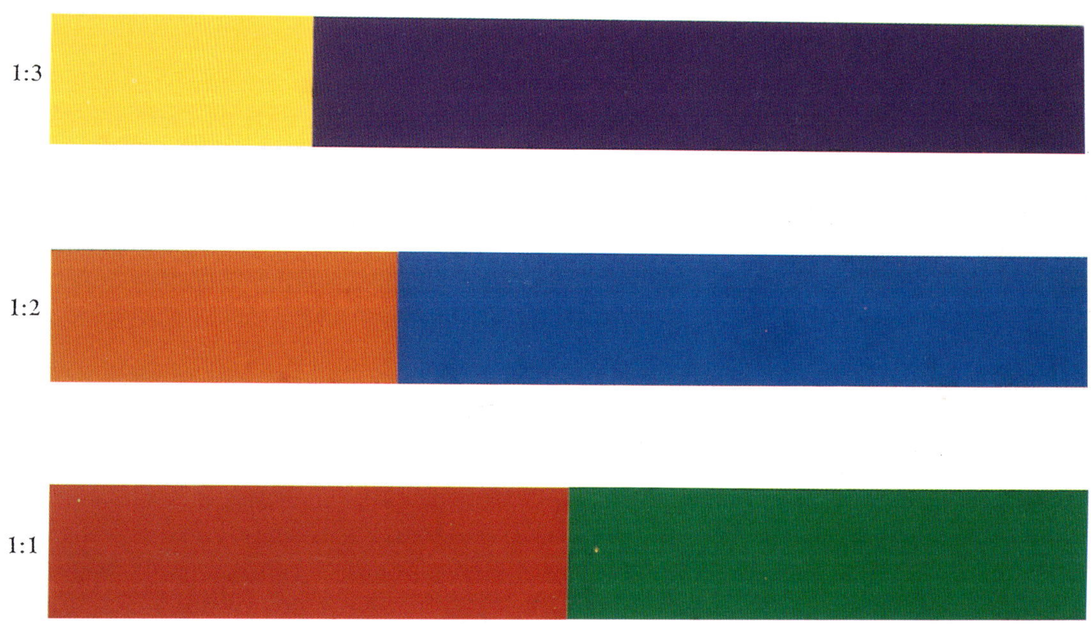

Figure 3-14 Harmonious Proportions of Complementary Hues

In setting these figures into harmonious areas, it is necessary to work with reciprocals. Thus, if yellow is three times as light as violet, it must occupy only a third of the space occupied by violet in a design in order to produce comfortable, stable, harmonious effects (figure 3-13). Needless to say these figures are qualitative and only represent approximations, but the effects produced—especially to the sensitized eye—are quite reliable.

If reciprocals are used to replace the original values assigned by Goethe, the harmonious relationships become quite easy to see: yellow = 3, orange = 4, red = 6, green = 6, blue = 8, and violet = 9. The visual proportions that would effect a balance of complements are shown in figure 3-14. Other harmonies may be produced based not on complementarity but on the value of one to another; for example, yellow:orange = 3:4, yellow:red = 3:6, yellow:blue = 3:8, and so on. Remember that these figures are only valid for hue relationships. If tints, shades, or tones are used, or if other qualities of hues are varied, the effect loses its quiet, stable state and becomes expressive.

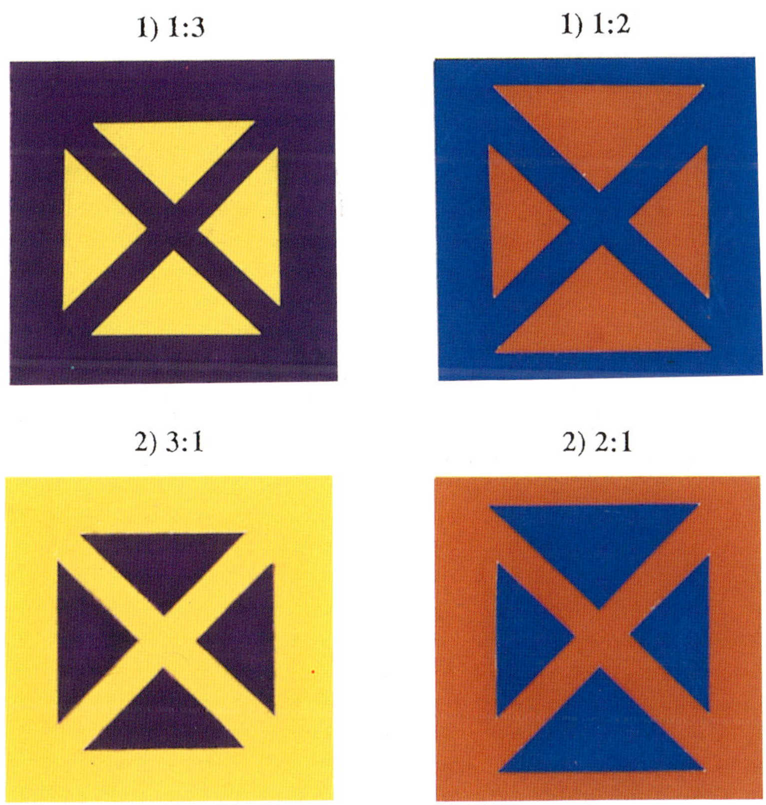

Figure 3-15 Altering Color Impact by Reversing Harmonious Proportions

This concept of complementarity represents only one way of solving problems of color harmony and balance. Artists and designers often originate ideas to fit expressive needs, and disharmony may be more relevant. If the contrast of proportion is reversed, a very different color expression—one of discord and discomfort—results (figure 3-15 and figure 3-16).

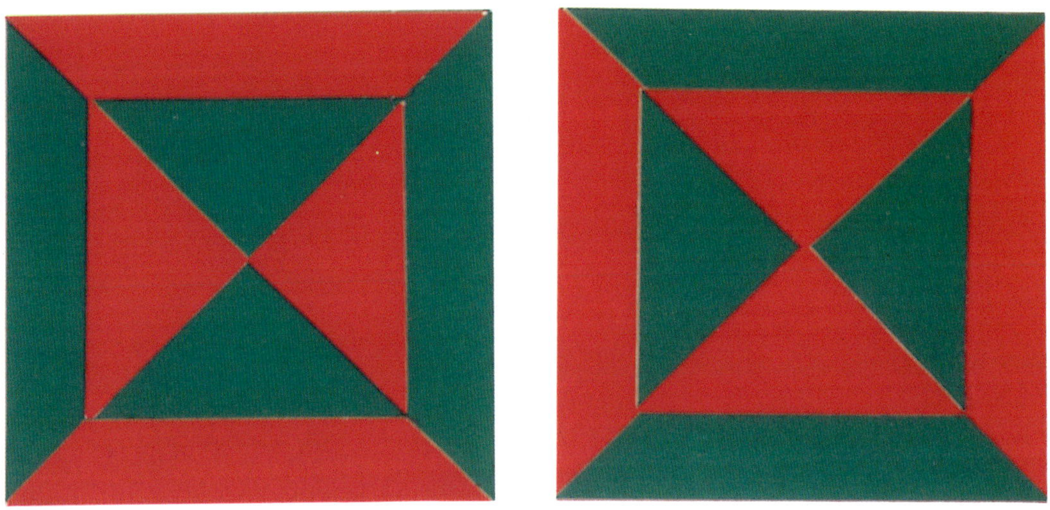

Figure 3-16 Altering Visual Sensation by Reversing Red and Green

4 COLOR CONTRASTS AND EFFECTS

When one color is placed next to another, or when a small area of one color is placed on a large area of another, things start happening. Both colors seem to have changed or to be in the process of changing. Certainly the relationship between colors is an active one in which subtle color shifts constantly occur and nothing is static. No wonder problems in color control seem so overwhelming at times. Fortunately, all apparent color effects are influenced by controllable light, an awareness of color contrast, and our own perception; consequently, each of these factors may be used to enhance or negate color expression. The essence of color control combines an understanding of light, color contrasts, and visual perception. With this knowledge and awareness, the aesthetic use of color results from a process of thought and manipulation rather than from intuition alone. This chapter addresses these issues.

Afterimages

In the middle of the nineteenth century, Michel-Eugene Chevreul (1786 – 1889), a chemist held in high esteem by the French government, was appointed Director of Dyes at the Gobelins Tapestry Works in Paris. His main concerns were with the visual effects that seemed to occur when solid areas of color were juxtaposed in the course of weaving. Chevreul was to make some insightful observations about how colors interact when placed side by side. Considering that in the nineteenth century his ideas were new and foreshadowed the disciplines of psychology and neurophysiology, his work seems all the more remarkable. The text he wrote on the harmony and contrast of color was widely read during his lifetime, became the guiding technical force behind the Impressionist and Neoimpressionist movements, and is still in print today. *

Chevreul concluded that color shifts are subjective phenomena; that is, we actually produce the sensation of color changes in our eye/brain apparatus, and since this is a matter of individual perception, not all color changes will be exactly the same for everyone. Later research substantiated his findings.

The apparent shifts in color quality that occur when colors are juxtaposed in various ways are now called *afterimages*, or afterim-

*M. E. Chevreul, *The Principles of Harmony and Contrast of Colors* (New York: Van Nostrand Reinhold, 1981).

age effects. Afterimages are not observed when the eye/brain is presented with all the wavelengths of visible light (that is, white light) and when the dominant value seen is a middle gray. However, when the eye/brain is subjected to a single wavelength or even to multiple wavelengths of light—for example, to strong reflected color(s)—but is not exposed to all wavelengths, the eye/brain "manufactures" the missing wavelength(s) in order to complete the visible spectrum and make a facsimile of white light. Afterimages can therefore be described as compensatory responses to very specific visual stimuli that serve to maintain a stable equilibrium of white light and a black-and-white balance of approximately 50 percent. Afterimages and the resulting color shifts are illusory, a fact that is sometimes quite difficult to accept because they seem so real.

As human beings, we experience different kinds of afterimages that relate to pattern, line, and movement, as well as to color and value; but the problems of color control are so involved with hue and value that this text will only address complementary and negative afterimages. The following principles are useful for observing color shifts:

1. HIGH-INTENSITY colors or hues stimulate or induce high-intensity afterimages (complementary afterimages).
2. LOW-INTENSITY colors induce low-intensity afterimages.
3. DARK VALUES induce light value afterimages (negative afterimages).
4. LIGHT VALUES induce dark value afterimages.

These color shifts are known as *simultaneous contrast* or *simultaneity*. They may be described as the result of viewing two colors (or values) at the same time while also seeing definite shifts (afterimages) in those colors.

In *The Principles of Harmony and Contrast of Colors,* Chevreul cites the following fourteen observations relating to contrast and afterimages:

1. Colors are shifted in appearance by their proximity to other colors (figure 4-1).
2. All colors seem lighter and more intense against black (figure 4-2).
3. All colors seem darker and less intense against white (figure 4-3).

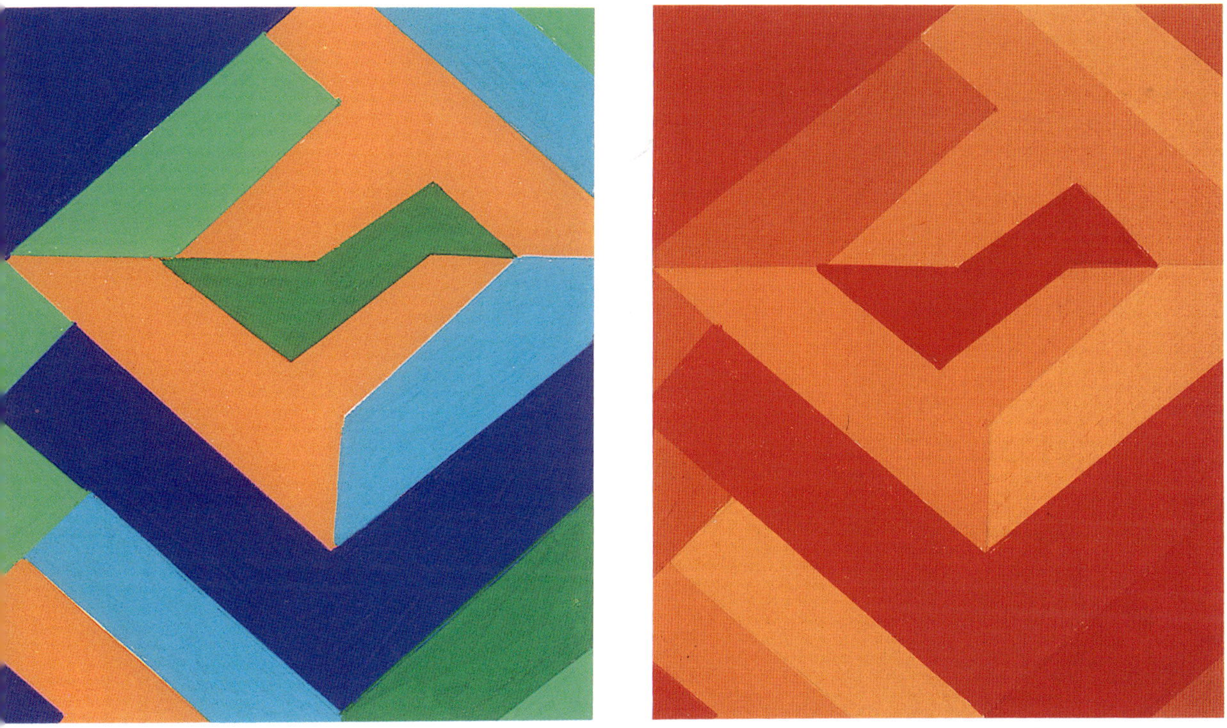

Figure 4-1 Changes in Appearance of Colors by Proximity to Other Colors

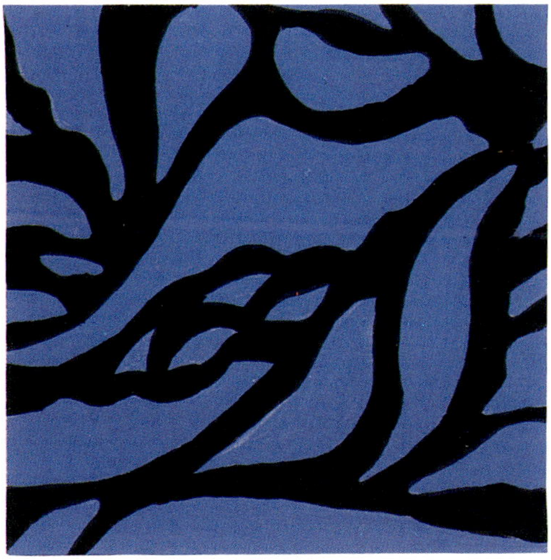

Figure 4-2 Increased Lightness and Intensity of Colors on Black

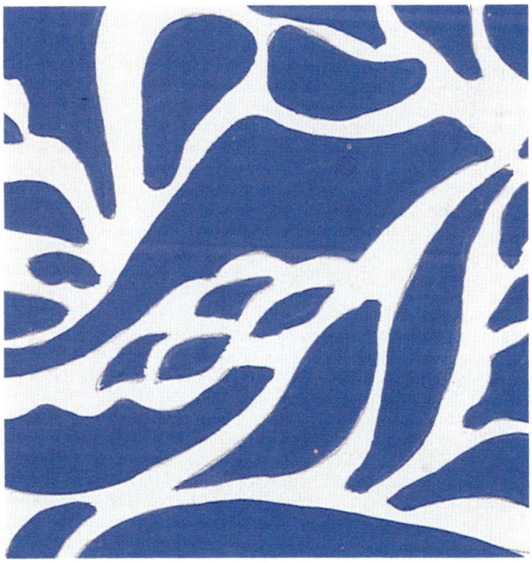

Figure 4-3 Increased Darkness and Diminished Intensity of Colors on White

Figure 4-4 Increased Darkness of Dark Colors and Values by Contrast on Light Colors and Values

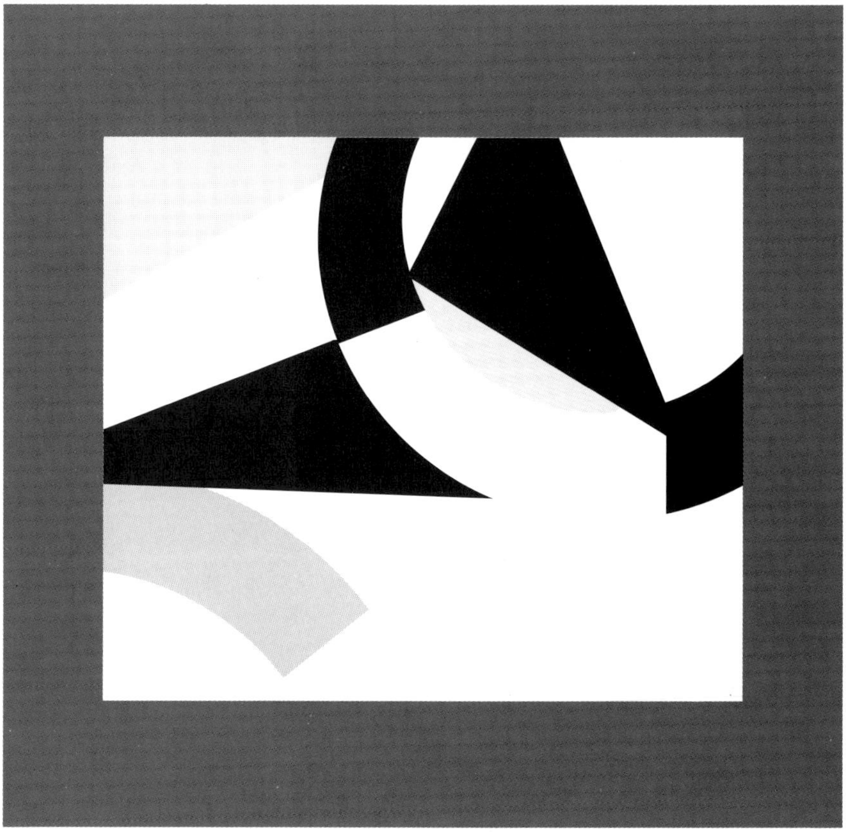

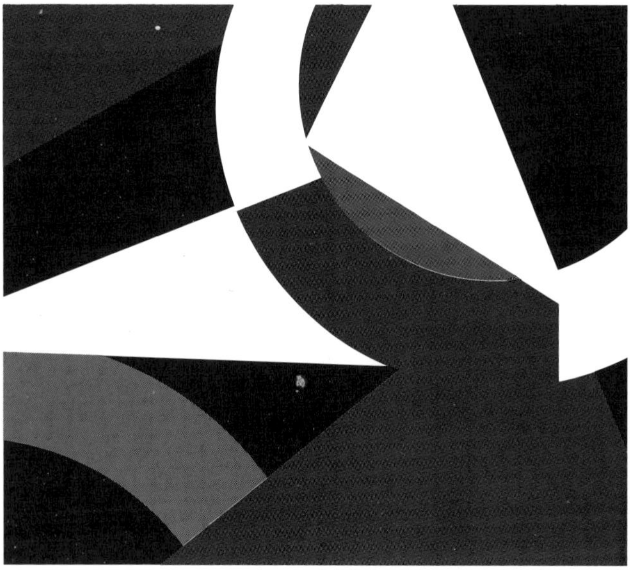

Figure 4-5 Increased Lightness of Light Colors and Values by Contrast on Dark Colors and Values

4. Dark colors and values on a background of light colors and values look darker than on a background of dark colors and values (figure 4-4).
5. Light colors and values on a background of dark colors and values look lighter than on a background of light colors and values (figure 4-5).
6. Colors are influenced in hue by adjacent colors, each coloring its neighbor with its own complement (figure 4-6).
7. If two complementary colors lie side by side, each seems more intense by contrast than it does by itself (figure 4-7).

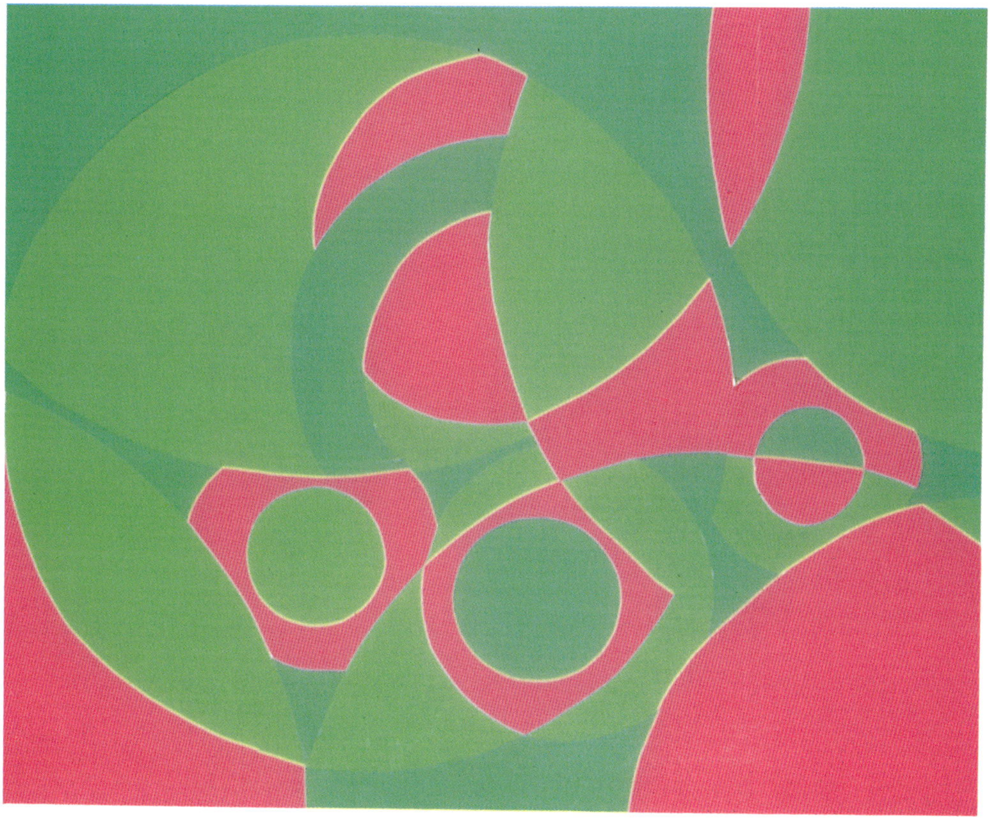

Figure 4-6 Influence on Hue by Adjacent Colors

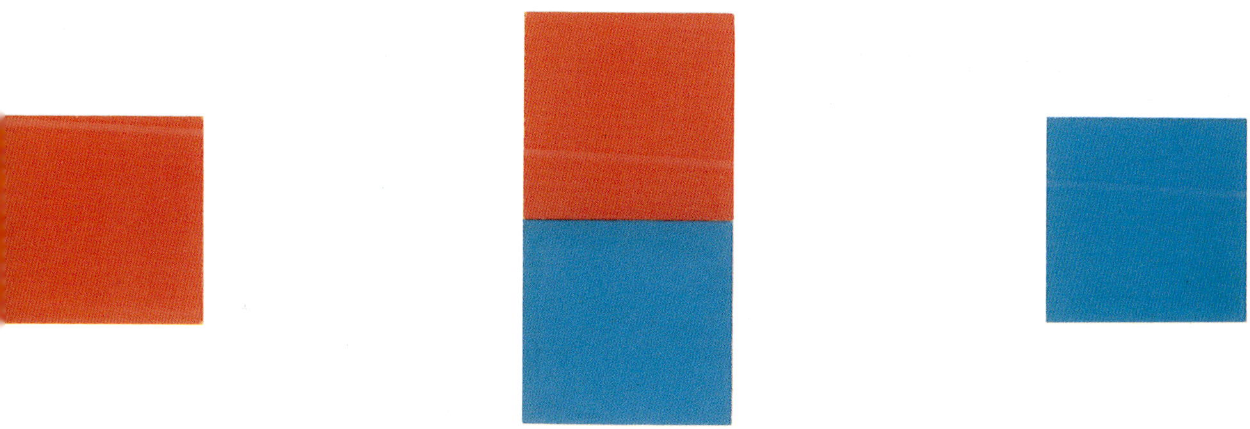

Figure 4-7 Increased Intensity of Two Complementary Colors seen Side by Side Instead of Separately

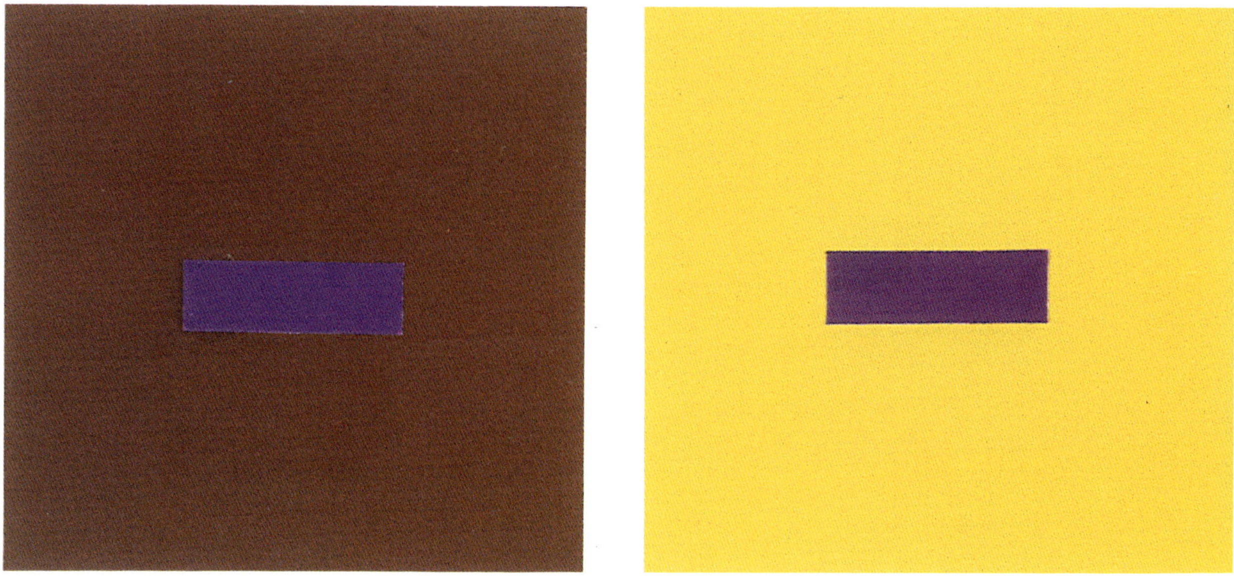

Figure 4-8 Diminished Intensity of Dark Colors on a Noncomplementary Dark Ground, versus on a Complementary Ground

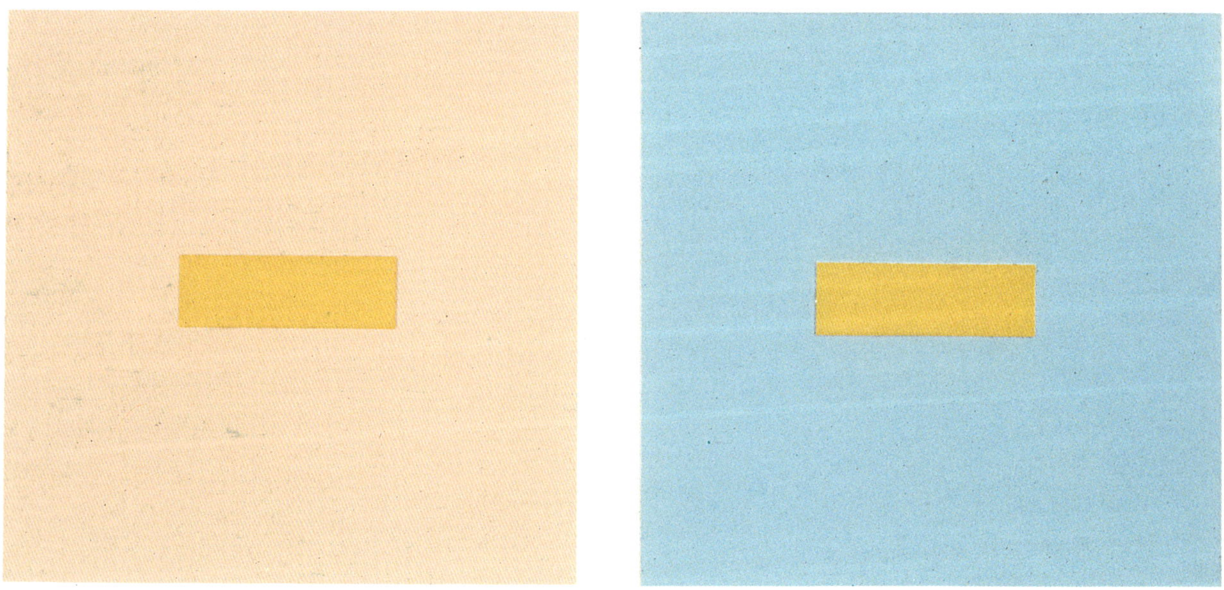

Figure 4-9 Diminished Intensity of Light Colors on a Noncomplementary Light Ground versus on a Complementary Ground

8. Dark colors on a dark background that is not complementary appear weaker or less intense than dark colors on a complementary background (figure 4-8).
9. Light colors on a light background that is not complementary appear weaker or less intense than light colors on a complementary background (figure 4-9).
10. An intense color against a dull or less intense color of the same hue further lessens the intensity of the dull color (figure 4-10).
11. When an intense color is used against a less intense color, the contrast is strongest when the latter is complementary (figure 4-11).

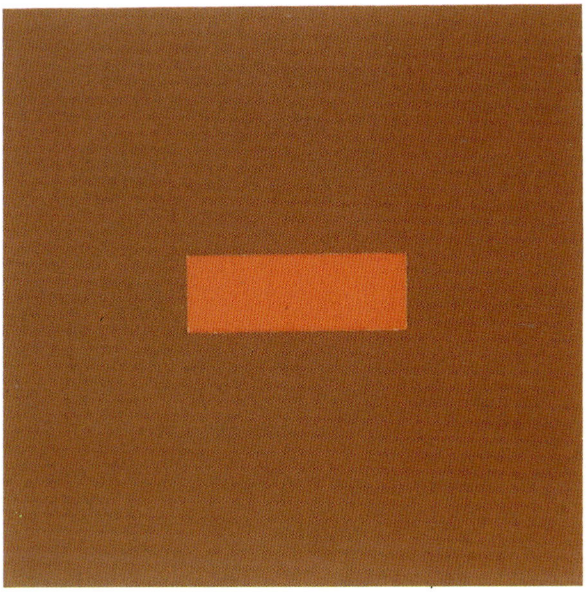

Figure 4-10 Further Diminution of the Intensity of a Weaker Color by Juxtaposition with an Intense Color of the Same Hue

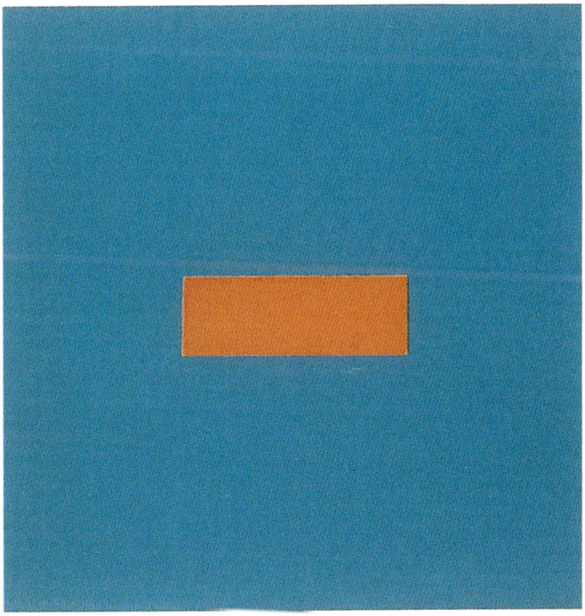

Figure 4-11 Maximum Contrast of an Intense Color Juxtaposed with a Less Intense but Complementary Color

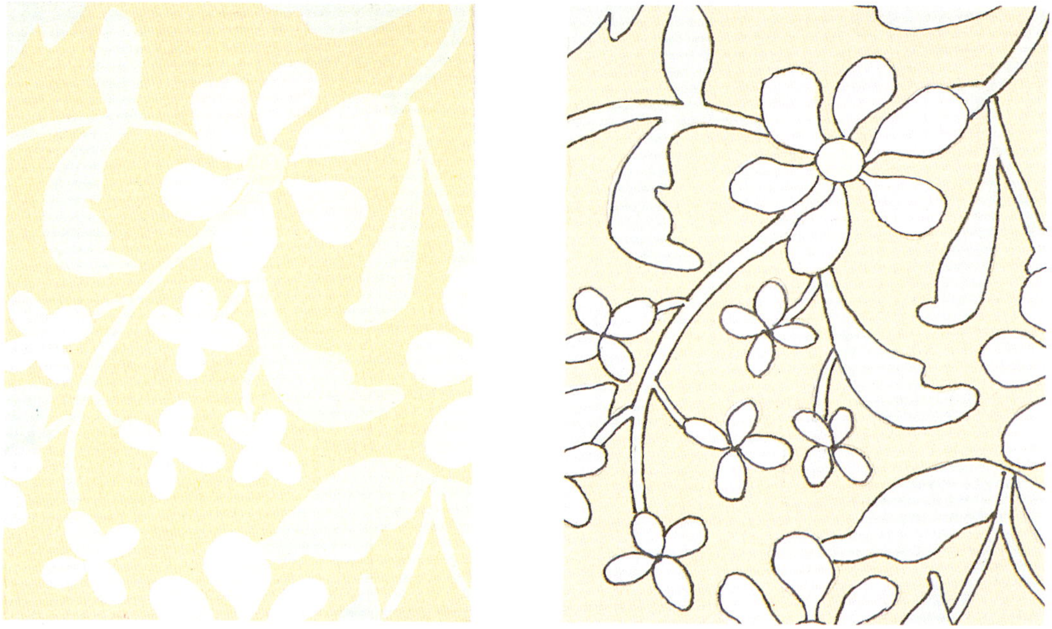

Figure 4-12 Strengthening Light Colors on Noncomplementary Light Grounds by Bounding Them with Narrow Bands of Black or Complementary Colors

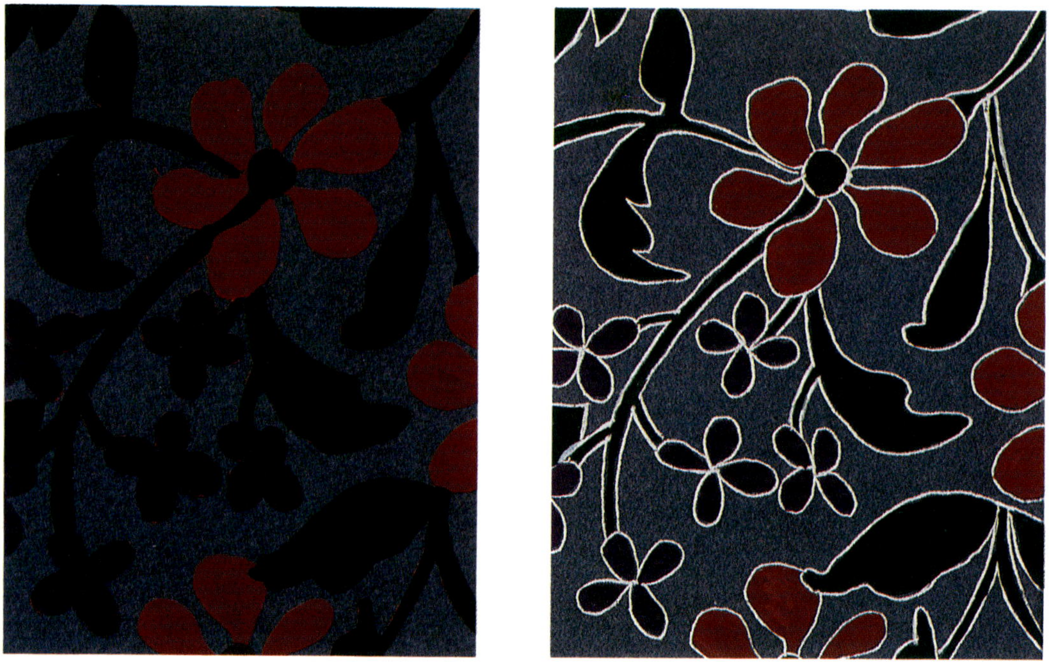

Figure 4-13 Strengthening Dark Colors on Noncomplementary Dark Backgrounds by Bounding Them with Narrow Bands of White or Light Complementary colors

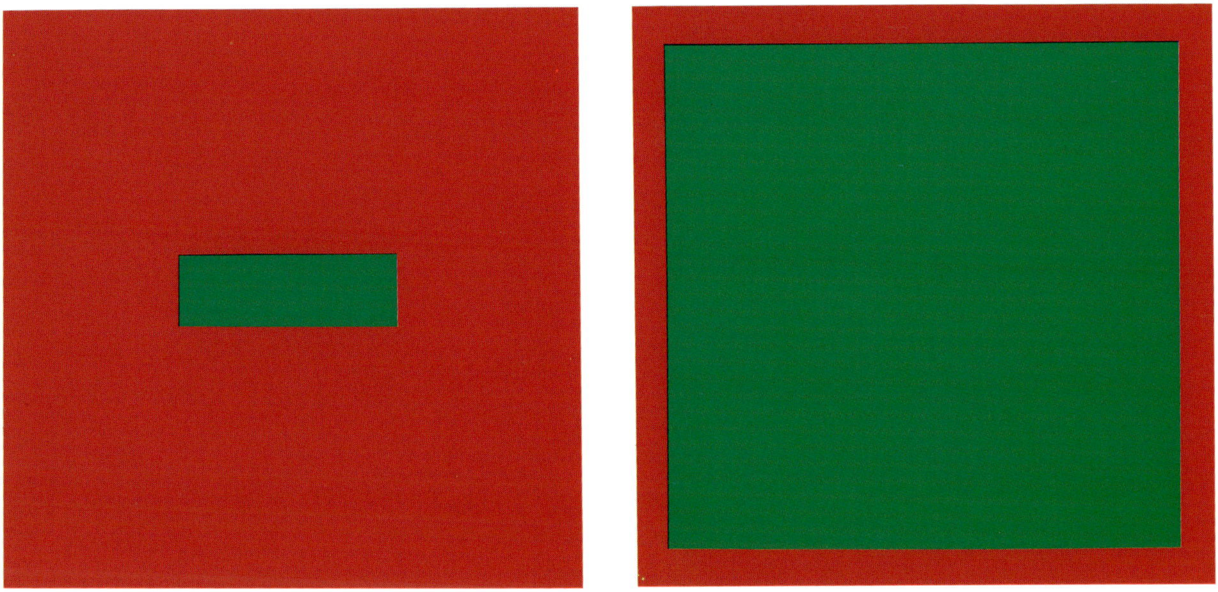

Figure 4-14 Maximum Afterimage Due to Equal-value Figure/Ground Colors and a Large Ground to Small Figure Relationship

12. Light colors on a light background that is not complementary can be strengthened if bounded by narrow bands of black or of complementary colors (figure 4-12).
13. Dark colors on a dark background that is not complementary can be strengthened if bounded by narrow bands of white or of light complementary colors (figure 4-13).
14. The strongest afterimage appears when figure and background (ground) colors have the same value and when the background is large in relation to the foreground figure (figure 4-14).

Successive Contrast

The simplest practical method of approaching afterimages is to look first at successive contrast. The difference between simultaneous and successive contrast lies in the fact that the former implies two things happening at the same time, whereas the latter involves the element of time or succession. For example, if a viewer stares at a sample of intense color for 10 to 15 seconds and then stares at a white board, an afterimage of the *light* (additive) complement of the original color will appear after a few seconds. In other words, if a blue color is stared at, the complement (and hence the afterimage), will be yellow, not orange; similarly, if a green color is stared at, the light complement will be magenta. This phenomenon is *successive contrast*; looking from the color area to a blank area enables the viewer to see the afterimage of the original color easily. The same procedure may be conducted with value. On the other hand, if a viewer stares at a dark value and then at a white board, the light value afterimage will not be observable to advantage. In this instance a board of high middle to middle value should be used to see the lighter value afterimage. Of course, the color and/or value of the board or paper used for seeing the induced afterimage will mix with the afterimage color, just as a glaze or wash influences the colors beneath it.

Using successive contrast, one can actually see what the afterimage of a specific hue, color, or value is. Only colors of relatively high intensity and values that are decidedly high or low will induce easily perceived afterimages. Other factors that affect the presence or staying quality of afterimages are the general health, age, and eye condition of the viewer. For example, certain drugs and degrees of stress actually change eye and brain chemistry, rendering the viewer incapable of perceiving a normal afterimage. Older people (70 to 90 years old) may also begin to experience problems with afterimage because of physiological changes that occur within the eye/brain with advanced age.

Simultaneous Contrast

Up to this point, the discussion has dealt with hue or complementary afterimage and value or negative afterimage as separate entities. Although it is easier to learn about them separately, complementary and negative changes are combined in the real experience of seeing afterimages. In simultaneous contrast or simultaneity, color shifts occur when two colors are seen side by side or when one is superimposed on another; both complementary and negative afterimages appear at the same time. It takes a little practice to adjust to the phenomenon, but visual understanding happens quickly. For example, if a viewer looks at a violet square whose value is approximately 80 percent, the viewer will at the same time perceive a light yellow-green square that has a value of approximately 20 percent. It is difficult to perceive the afterimage clearly unless there is a figure of a low-intensity color in the center of the violet to act as a window to the eye/brain, permitting the viewer to see the afterimage quite clearly. Again, afterimages have a transparent quality that makes them seem to float over colors in our vision, behaving in much the same manner as do transparent washes in watercolor or glazes in oil. In the case of the violet ground, a small gray figure at its center allows the viewer to see the afterimage shift of hue and value. If a color is neither dark nor light but falls near the middle of the value scale, however, the negative afterimage is hardly noticeable, while the complementary afterimage is dramatic—for example a green/magenta shift.

Simultaneous contrast, happily, can be manipulated to achieve a specific desired effect. The following methods can be used to reinforce or exaggerate afterimages:

1. Use large areas of complementary colors (figure 4-15). Even though all visible wavelengths of light are present, when the colors lie side by side, the eye does not scan rapidly enough to cancel the afterimages; the colors therefore reinforce each other by producing joint afterimages.

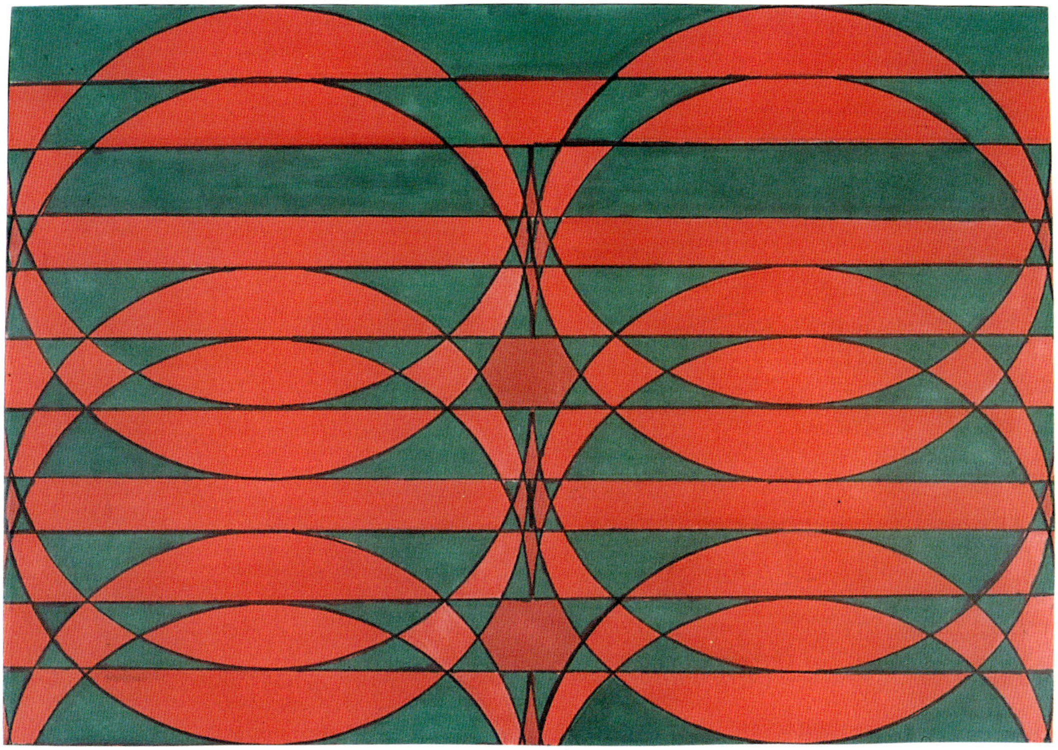

Figure 4-15 Reinforcing Simultaneity by Using Large Areas of Complementary Colors

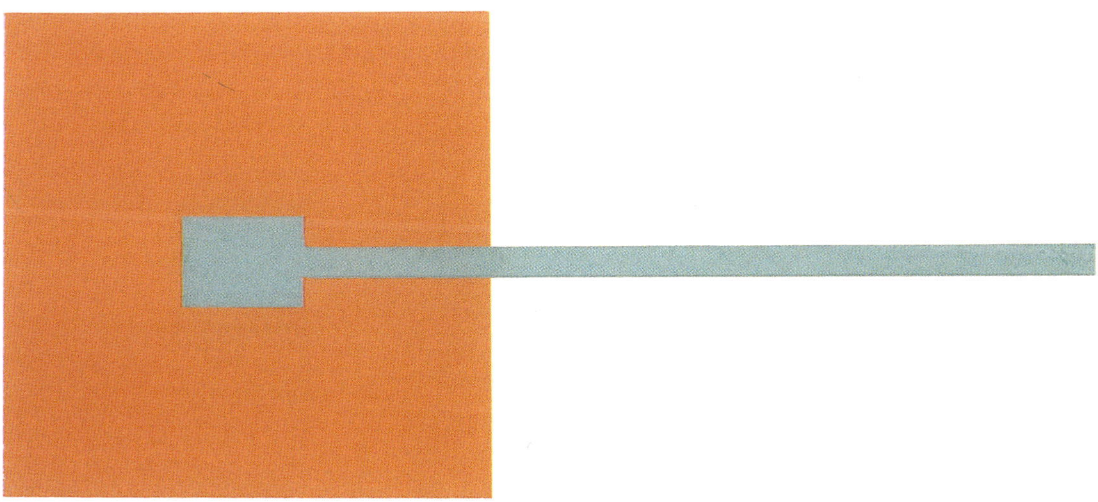

Figure 4-16 Reinforcing Simultaneity by Using Large High-intensity Grounds to Small Low-intensity Figures and Keeping the Value Similar

2. Use large high-intensity grounds to small low-intensity figures, keeping the values similar (figure 4-16).

3. Use a small amount of the afterimage color mixed with the figure color (figure 4-17). This is simple to do in the case of painting and mixing pigments. When working with papers or fabrics, choose a color that contains some of the afterimage color.

4. Use a complementary outline around a foreground figure (figure 4-18).

5. Use value contrast in color (figure 4-19).

6. Use a black background (figure 4-20).

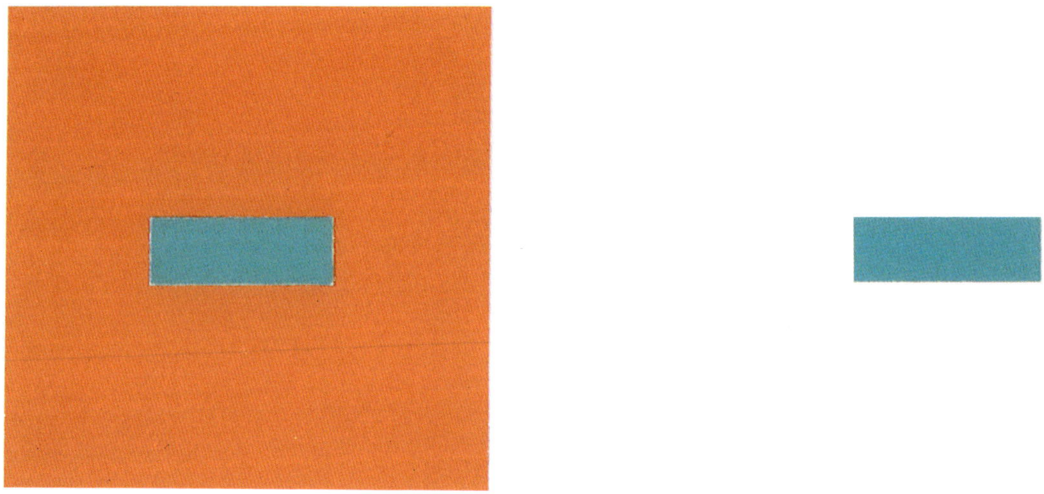

Figure 4-17 Reinforcing Simultaneity by Using a Small Amount of the Afterimage Color Mixed with the Figure Color

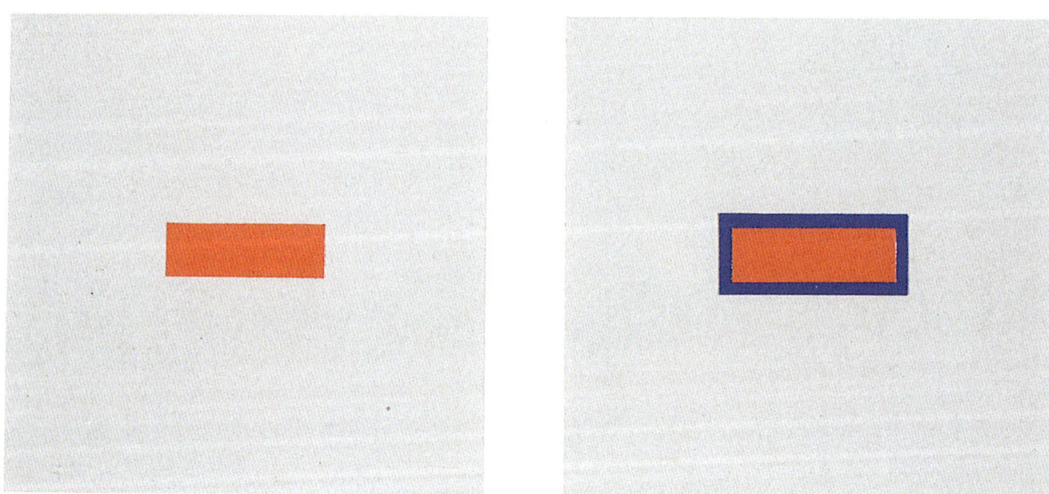

Figure 4-18 Reinforcing Simultaneity by Using a Complementary Outline Around a Foreground Figure

Figure 4-19 Reinforcing Simultaneity by Using Value Contrast in Color

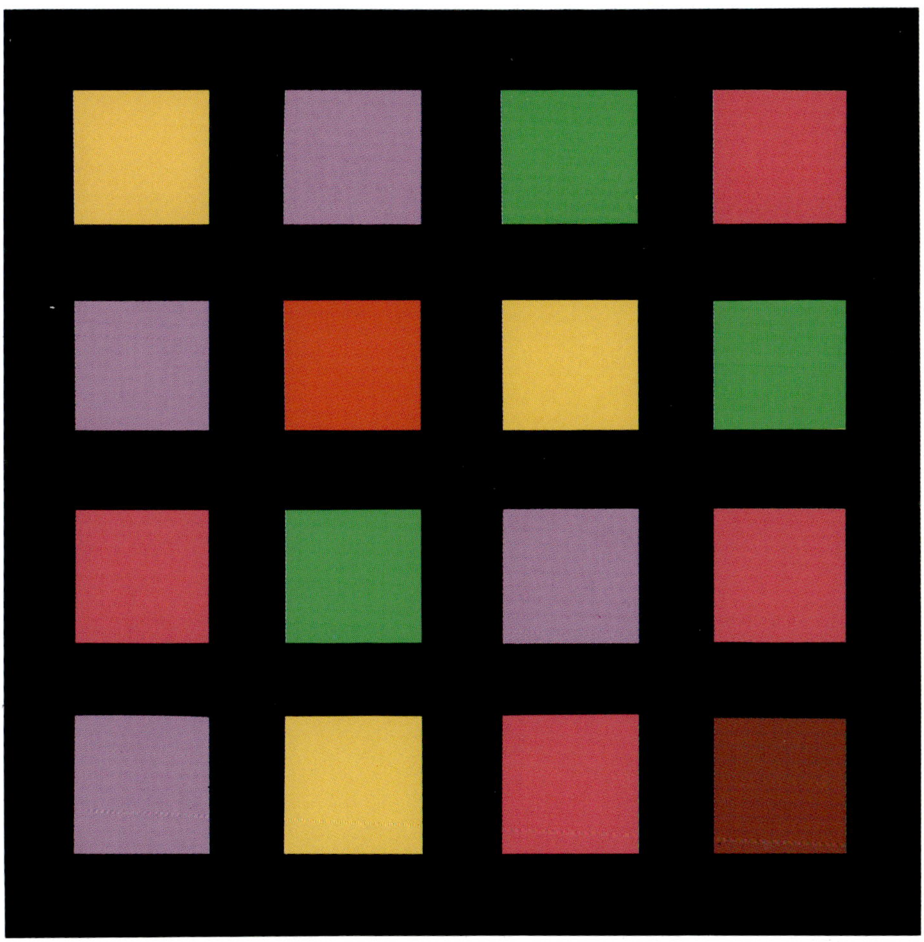

Figure 4-20
Reinforcing
Simultaneity
by Using a
Black Background

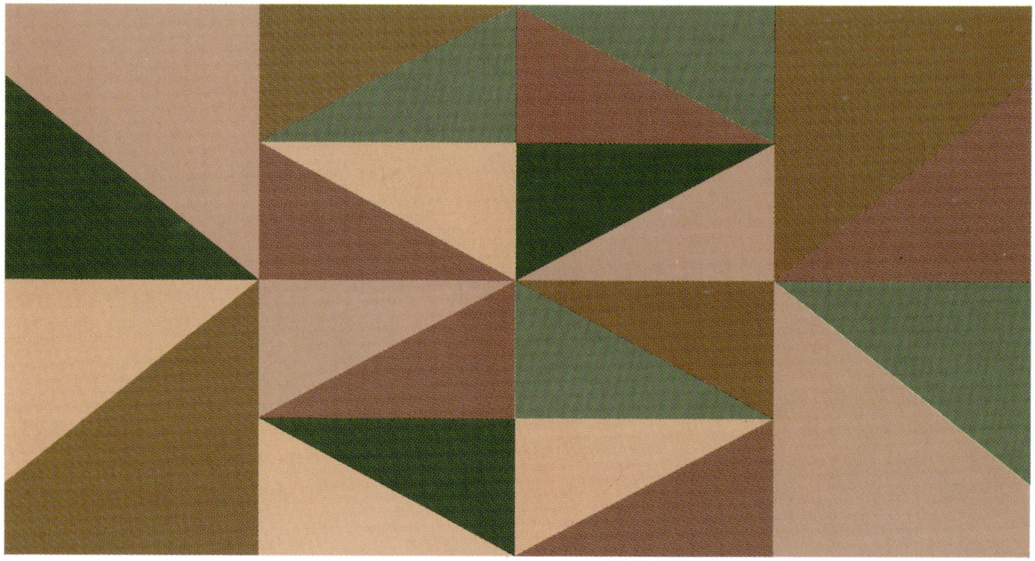

Figure 4-21 Reducing Simultaneity by Using Closely Related Values and Low-intensity Colors

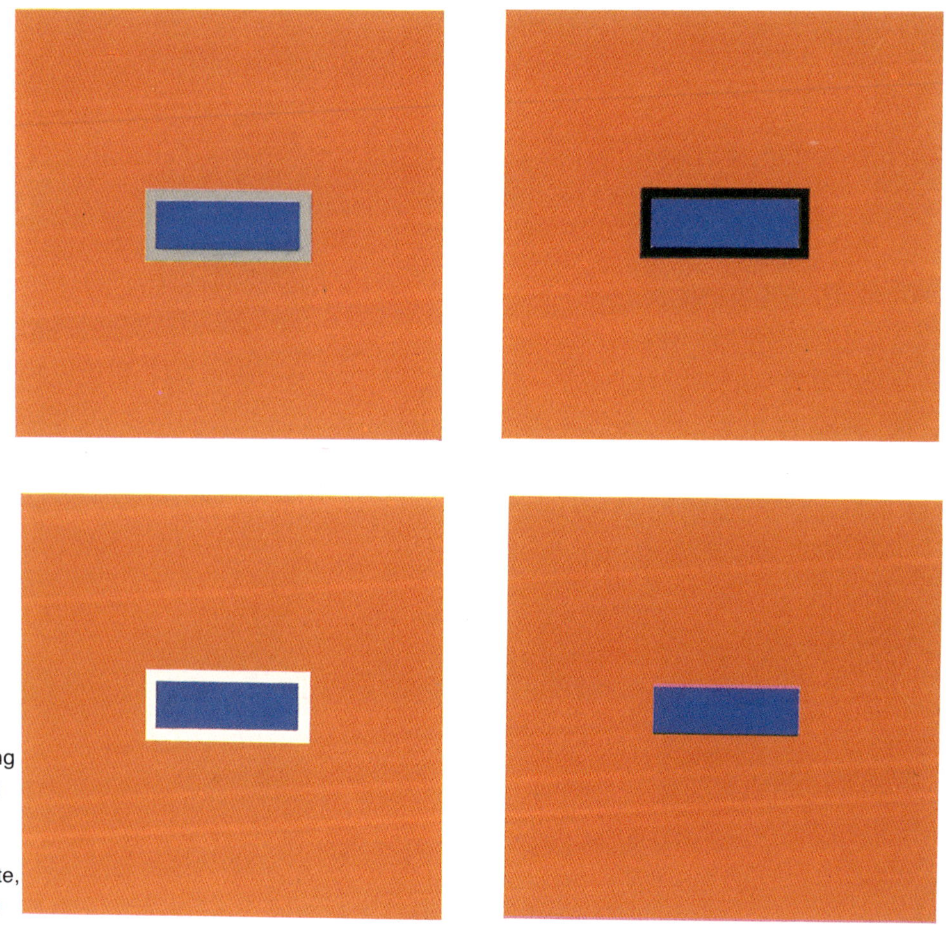

Figure 4-22 Reducing Simultaneity by Using an Outline Around a Figure That Is a Value (Preferably White, Black, or Middle Gray)

Keep in mind that the greater the contrast between any or all of the color properties, the more dramatic the simultaneity, except in method 2, where the values are kept similar to maximize the complementary afterimage.

The following methods can be used to reduce or cancel afterimages:

1. Use closely related values and low-intensity colors (figure 4-21).
2. Use an outline around a figure that is a value, preferably white, black, or middle gray (figure 4-22).
3. Use a small area of white and/or black in a design (figure 4-23). A large area of such color, however, tends to produce a negative afterimage.
4. Use a background of white (figure 4-24). This tends to cool the colors in a design; and although simultaneous contrast does occur, the dark afterimage reduces color impact and therefore reduces simultaneity.

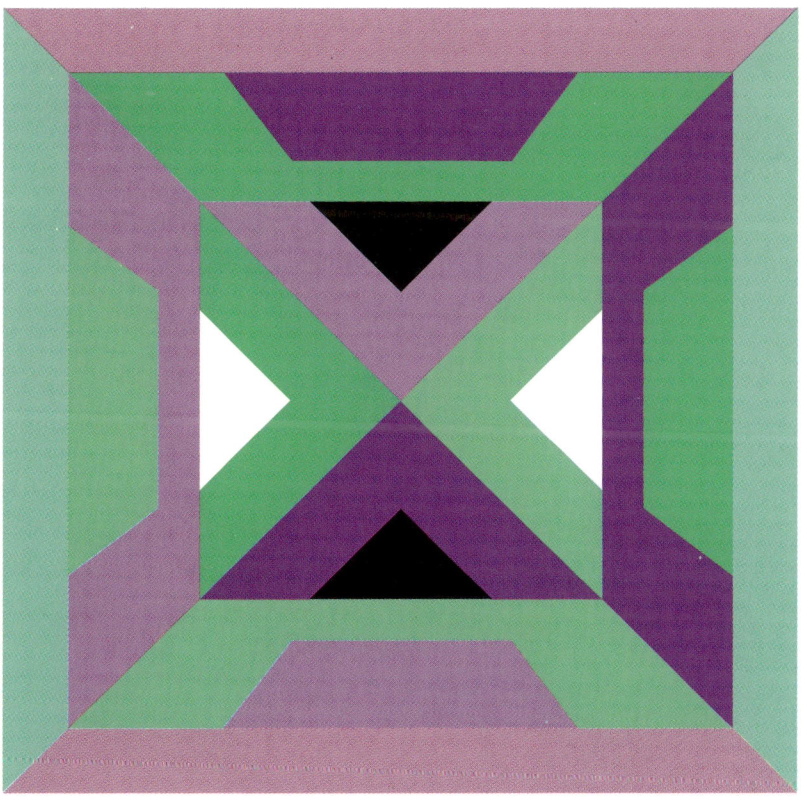

Figure 4-23 Reducing Simultaneity by Using a Small Area of White and/or Black in a Design

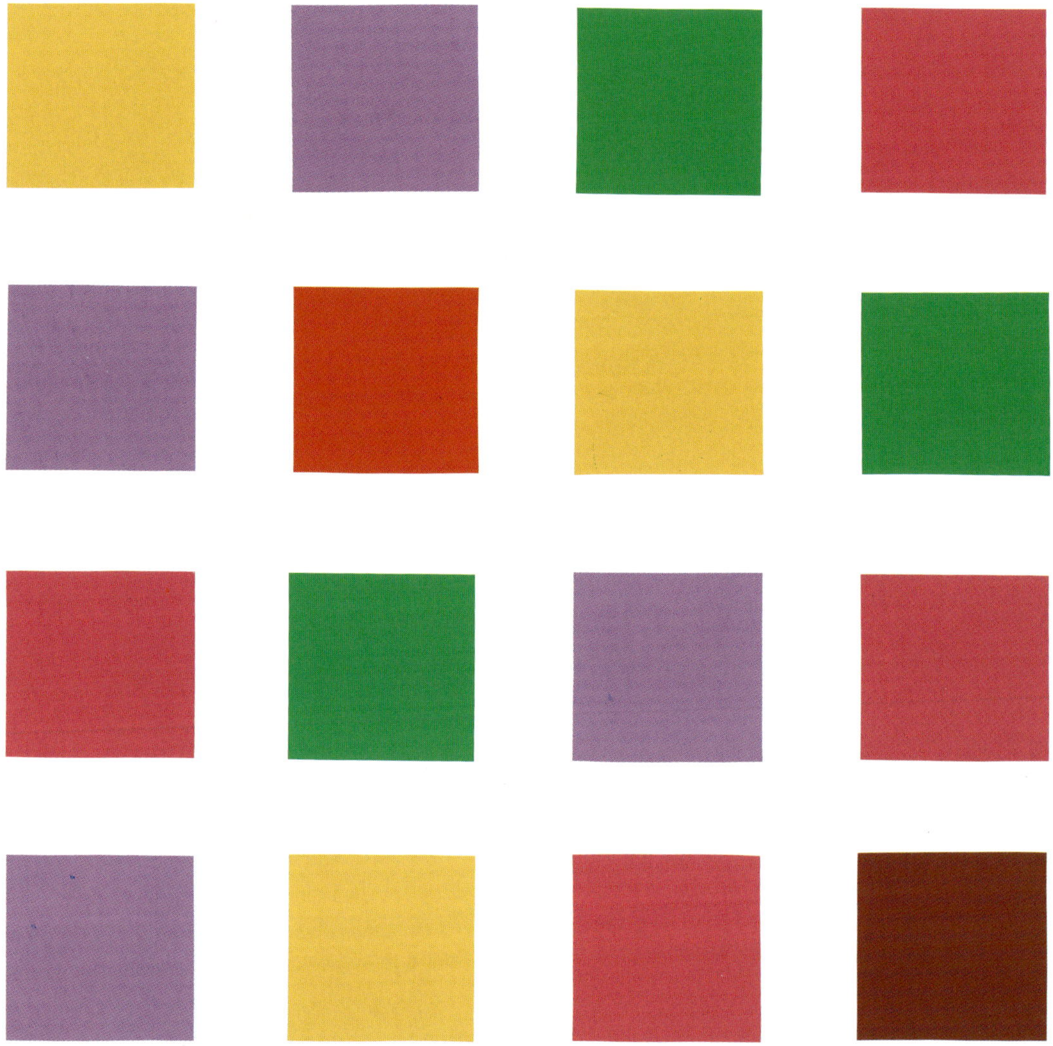

Figure 4-24 Reducing Simultaneity by Using a White Background

5. Use a small-scale pattern to break up larger areas of color (figure 4-25).
6. Use a small amount (shape) of complementary color in a design (figure 4-26).

Simultaneity occurs all the time, even when the afterimage is too low or indistinct to be perceived consciously. Thus, whether we perceive an identifiable afterimage or not, all colors tend to shift another color toward its own complement, and each color is changed to some degree.

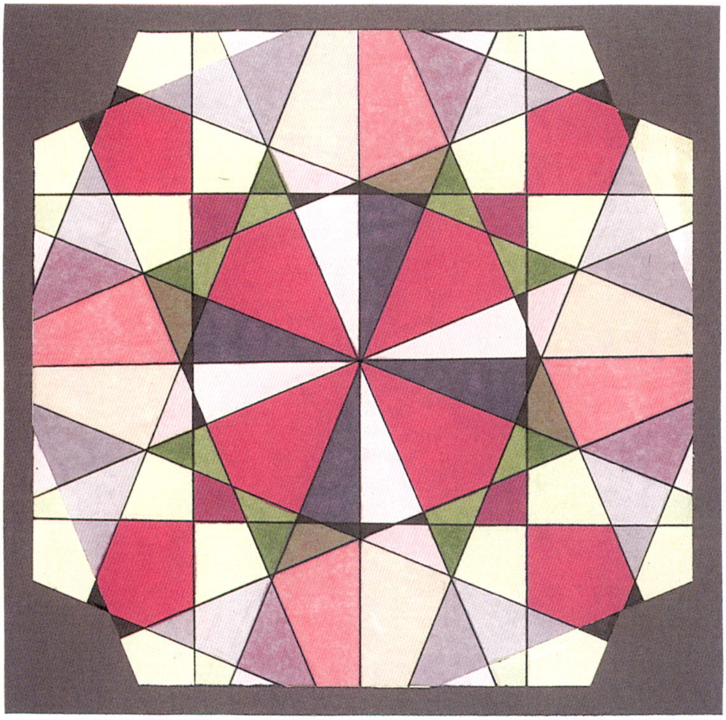

Figure 4-25 Reducing Simultaneity by Using a Small-scale Pattern to Break up Larger Areas of Color

Figure 4-26 Reducing Simultaneity by using a Small Amount (Shape) of Complementary Color in a Design

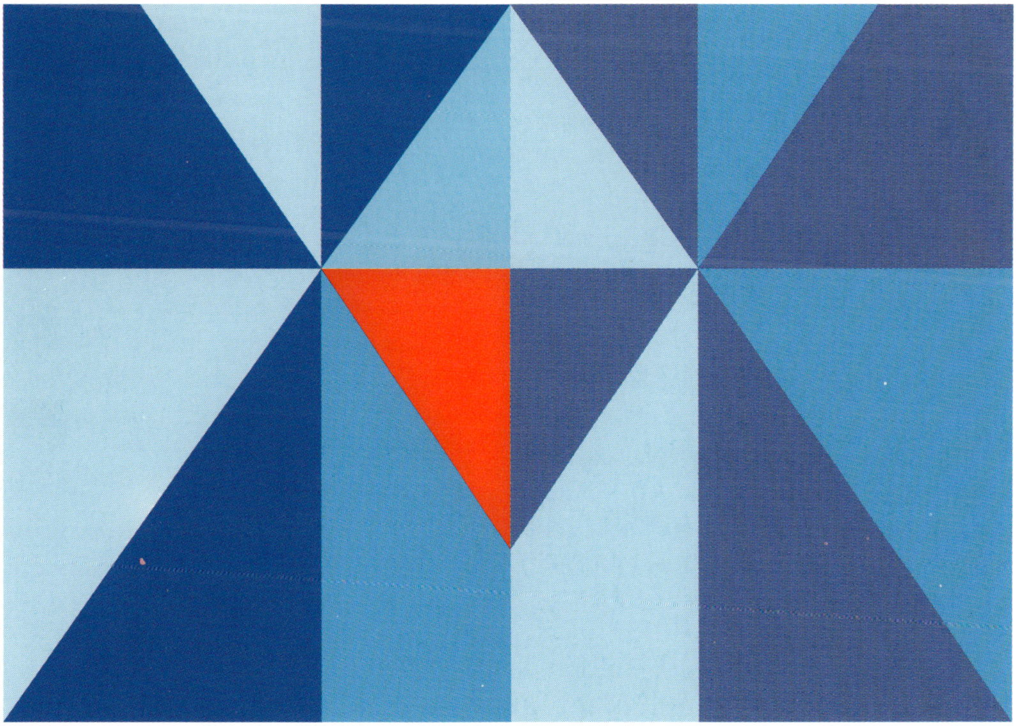

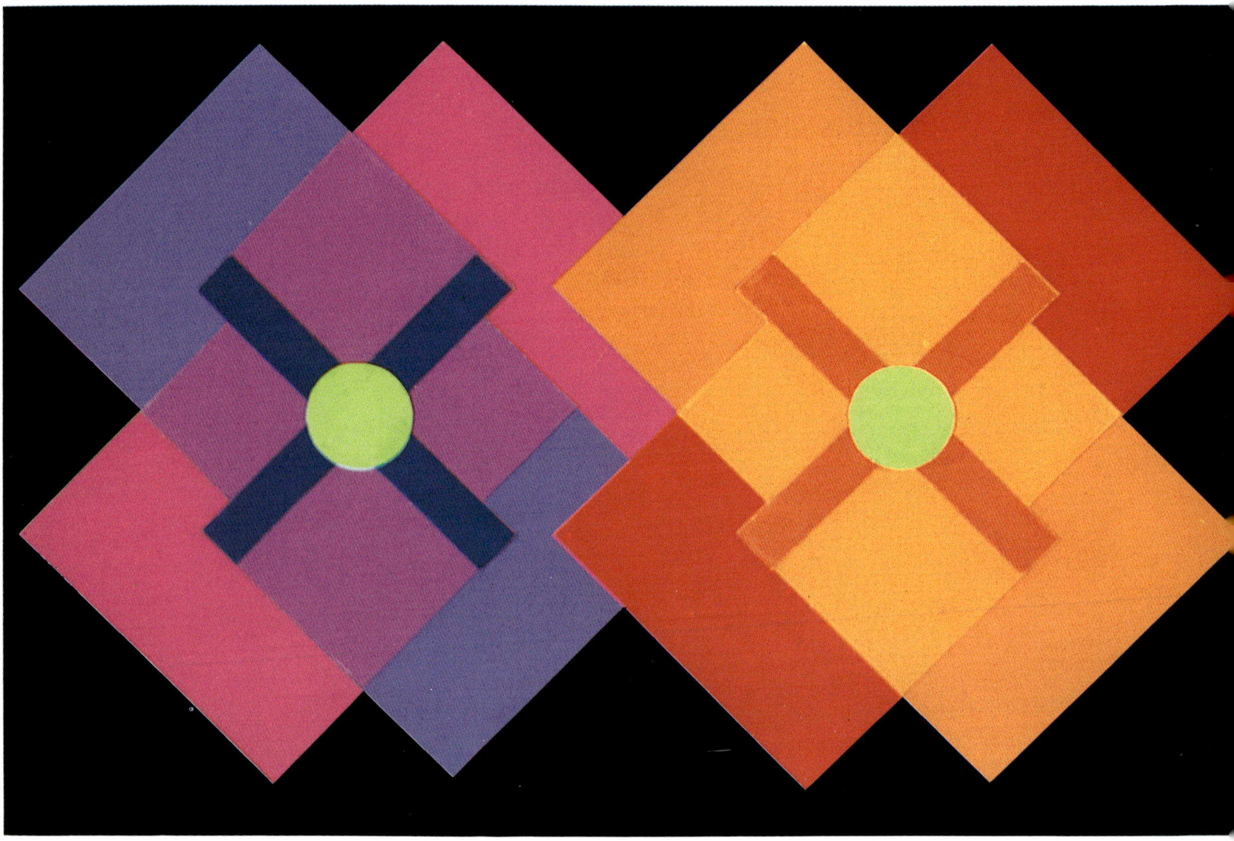

Figure 4-27 Temperate Colors Shifted from Warm to Cool by Simultaneity

Contrast of Temperature

Warm/cool contrasts are straightforward and can be extremely expressive when used to produce a spatial or psychological impact. Color effects become a little less clear when temperate hues or colors (those that fall between green/yellow and red/violet on the hue circle) are used. Because temperate colors are composed of a primary and a secondary color each, they lend themselves readily to manipulation with simultaneity. Figure 4-27 offers an excellent example of how a temperate color may appear to be warm and/or cool at the same time. In the case of the red/violet, when an orange ground, a yellow/orange ground, or a ground that contains several different oranges is used, the afterimage stimulated will be in the blue range. Hence, a blue will float over the center figure, enhancing the blue in the red/violet. If another figure of red/

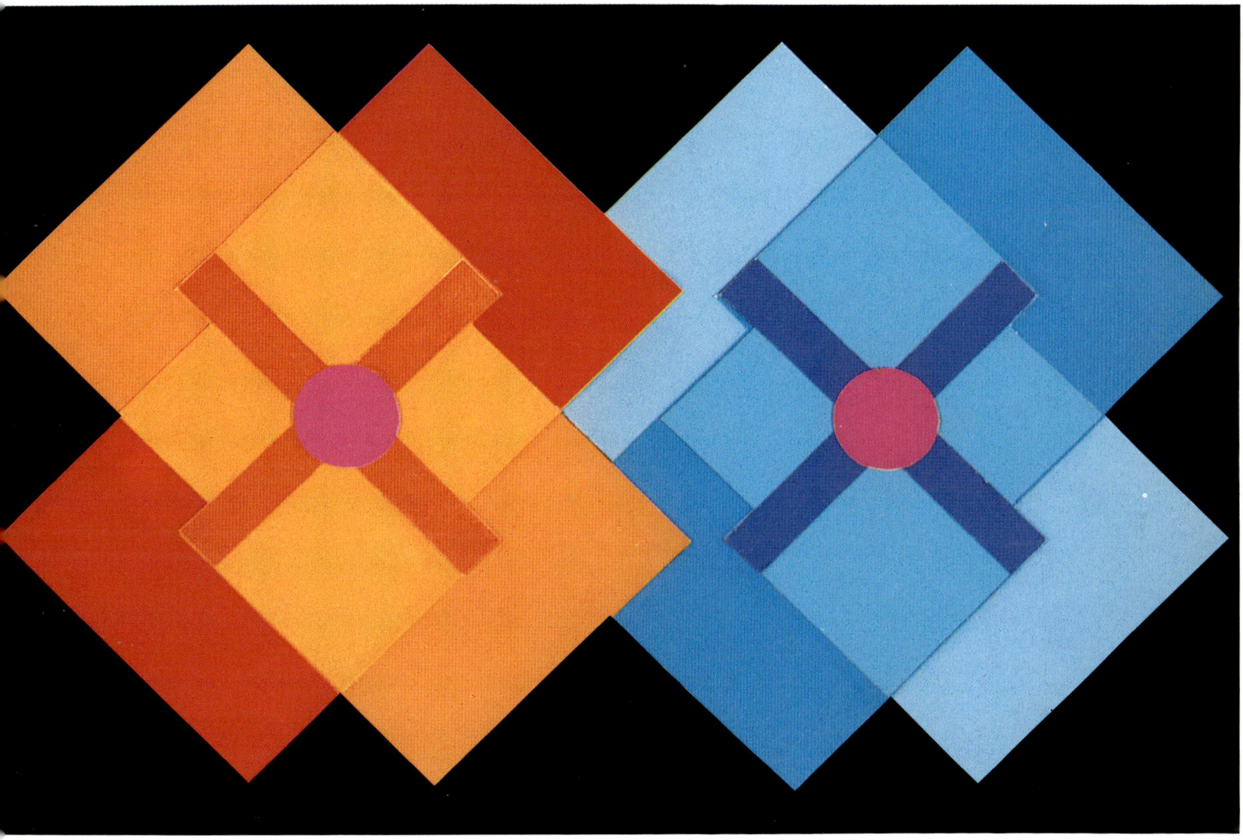

violet is surrounded by blues and/or blue greens, the afterimage will be orange/yellow or red, depending on the amount of green present, and this warm afterimage will enhance the red aspect of the color. As a result, the red/violet will appear warmer and quite different from the red/violet with a blue afterimage. Although the colors are the same, they appear very different. Exactly the same technique works with the yellow/green figures. One ground enhances the yellow content of the hue by stimulating a yellow afterimage, while the other enhances the green or the blue of the green, thereby making the same color look warm and cool at the same time.

A strong, visible afterimage has the ability to change color perception of temperate hues and colors quite remarkably.

5 COLORANT MIXING

A *colorant* is any substance that, by its chemical or physical nature, imparts the sensation of color to the viewer. A color either selectively reflects and absorbs or transmits specific wavelengths of light. Pigments, dyes, and inks are either naturally or chemically produced colorants that fall into three categories of permanence: permanent; semipermanent, with some instability and fading; and fugitive, with severe fading rather rapidly. The most reliable manufacturers of artists' materials identify the permanence of their materials on their products and charts.

Mixtures of colored lights do not behave in the same manner as mixtures of colorants. When colored light is mixed, the color of the light produced represents the combination of wavelengths of light. Thus, the combination of all three light primaries—blue-violet, red-orange, and green—*in equal proportion* produces white light. This is called *additive mixing*.

Subtractive mixing occurs when pigments, dyes, inks, or transparent layers of colors (such as a series of transparent colored acetate sheets) are superimposed on one another. This chapter is about subtractive mixing and about the production of new vocabularies of color by mixing artists' pigments or paints.

A Mixing Technique

There are probably as many different approaches to mixing paint as there are visual artists working in the field. However, not all of these methods lend themselves to the preparation of color samples for future reference. The technique described here for making color samples is strongly recommended because it works easily and well.

The following materials are needed:

- A trowel-shaped painting knife at least 3 inches long and approximately 1 inch across at its widest point (figure 5-1). Do not use a palette knife; it is neither as flexible nor as comfortable to work with as a painting knife.
- A reliable brand of acrylic paint such as Bocour's Aquatec, Permanent Pigments Liquitex, the products of Grumbacher, or any other major manufacturer of quality artists' materials. Avoid the small companies and very inexpensive paints. If possible, also obtain a color chart from the store or

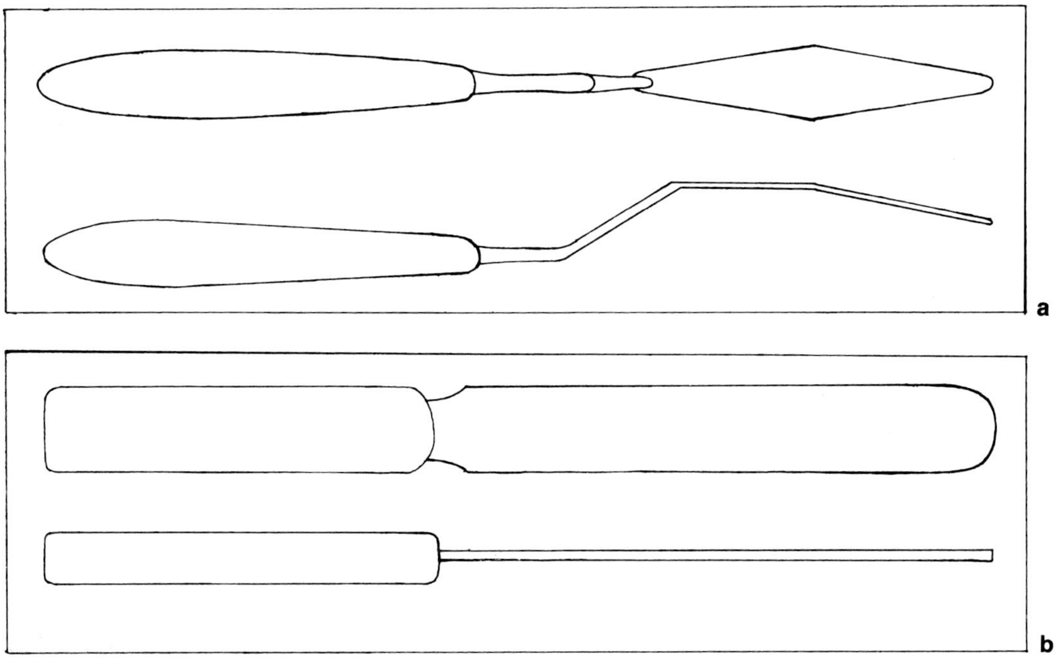

Figure 5-1 Painting Knife (a) and Palette Knife (b)

directly from the company, to keep records of the colors used for various mixes.

- A large (at least an 11- × 14-inch) disposable palette to aid in keeping mixtures clean. The top sheet may be torn off and thrown away or recycled as the mixtures demand. It is not a good idea to mix more than two colors in the same area, because "skins" of paint begin to dry and then knifing out a sample to a textureless surface becomes impossible.
- A pad of two-ply bristol board of any convenient size, with a vellum or plate finish. A very smooth, glossy surface is acceptable, too, but the knifing technique lends itself better to a rougher surface.
- A metal straightedge at least 12 inches long and cutting tools such as mat knife, scissors, or X-acto—whatever is most comfortable to use.
- A can of rubber cement.
- A large, bound sketchbook (11 × 14 or larger) to keep the color charts and samples in.
- Miscellaneous items for painting, including paper towels and/or rags and a large container for water (figure 5-2).

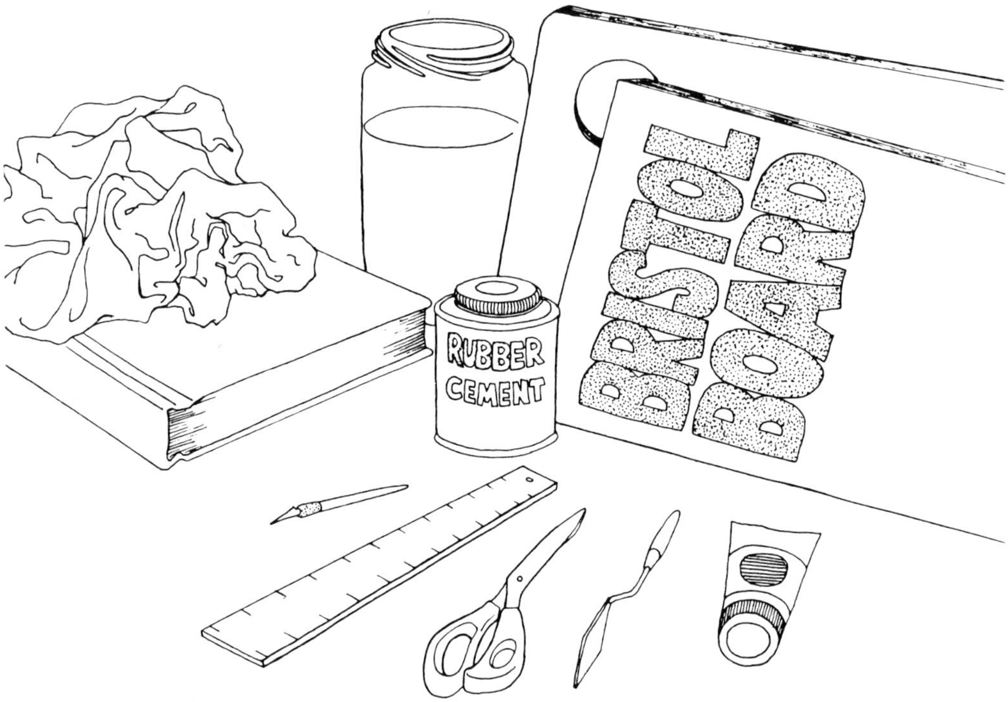

Figure 5-2 Painting Supplies for Colorant Mixing

Acrylic paints are recommended for their ease of handling, their rapid drying, and their easy cleanup. If oil colors are used, the mixing technique remains the same, but cleanup is more involved and drying time is quite a bit longer. The best rule of thumb is to remember that color samples and scales provide more information when they are produced in the medium most often used by the designer/artist. A person who regularly produces work in gouache, for example, probably should produce reference colors in that medium. If there is any latitude, however, acrylic paints are probably the best choice.

Oils are the only paints other than encaustic (which is *not* recommended) that require a specific solvent for cleanup and thinning. All other paints use water. Either turpentine or mineral spirits (also known as odorless paint thinner) may be used for these purposes with oil paints. Mineral spirits is preferable to turpentine because it is less expensive, causes fewer skin allergies, and evaporates completely. Both mineral spirits and turpentine may be combined with linseed oil and/or varnish to thin paints and to use for cleanup.

When oil paints dry, they retain the color they had when wet. Water-based paints, for the most part, dry down; that is, they dry to a slightly darker value than they had when wet. For this reason it is necessary to match trial swatches of colors after they have dried.

Figure 5-3 illustrates the method of paint mixing recommended in this text. Several basic suggestions should be kept in mind:

1. Develop clean habits of mixing. For instance, keep the palette area organized, and produce few mixes per sheet. If a standard wood, plastic, or glass palette is used, be sure to clean it often.

2. Use only a good painting knife when mixing actual colors. Brushes are very difficult to clean completely. Paint creeps up into the ferrule (the crimped metal piece that holds the hair or bristles onto the handle) and then moves out into new mixes, contaminating them.

3. Use enough paint to give the quantity of mix needed to knife out a sample. When too little paint is used, a smooth opaque film simply cannot be obtained.

4. The consistency of the paint is important. A mixture resembling very soft butter knifes out well. Add a little water (or thinner) to the mix to achieve the desired consistency. If the paint is too thick, the resulting paint film will be too dense and will lower the apparent intensity or brilliance of the mix. If the paint is too thin, however, the color will not be opaque and will not spread evenly, giving misleading results.

5. The colors *must* be blended completely and uniformly, so that streaks of unmixed or partially mixed color are not present and value changes do not occur. The technique demands a little patience in the beginning, but it is well worth the effort and becomes relatively simple with practice.

When the mixture is complete and the consistency is acceptable, the paint should be loaded onto the knife and spread as evenly as possible over the bristol board. The desired result is a textureless, evenly layered paint film of uniform thickness, allowing the viewer to assess the color without having to deal with variables of texture.

After the sample is dry, a 1- × 3-inch piece (smaller if the color swatch demands it) is cut from the knifed-out area and either laid directly on top of the color being matched or set aside and used in a scale. When all the steps in a scale are finished, rubber-cement them into place side by side.

Every color has the characteristic of changing another color to a greater or lesser degree. This feature is known as the *tinctorial power* or *strength* of the color. For example, the tinctorial power of dark colors is greater than that of light ones. A small amount of violet added to yellow will change the character of the yellow markedly; a small amount of yellow added to violet will have little or no evident effect. A person who ignores the concept of tinctorial power can easily wind up wasting a lot of paint to achieve mixtures of a desired color. If a light color is added to a dark color to obtain an inter-

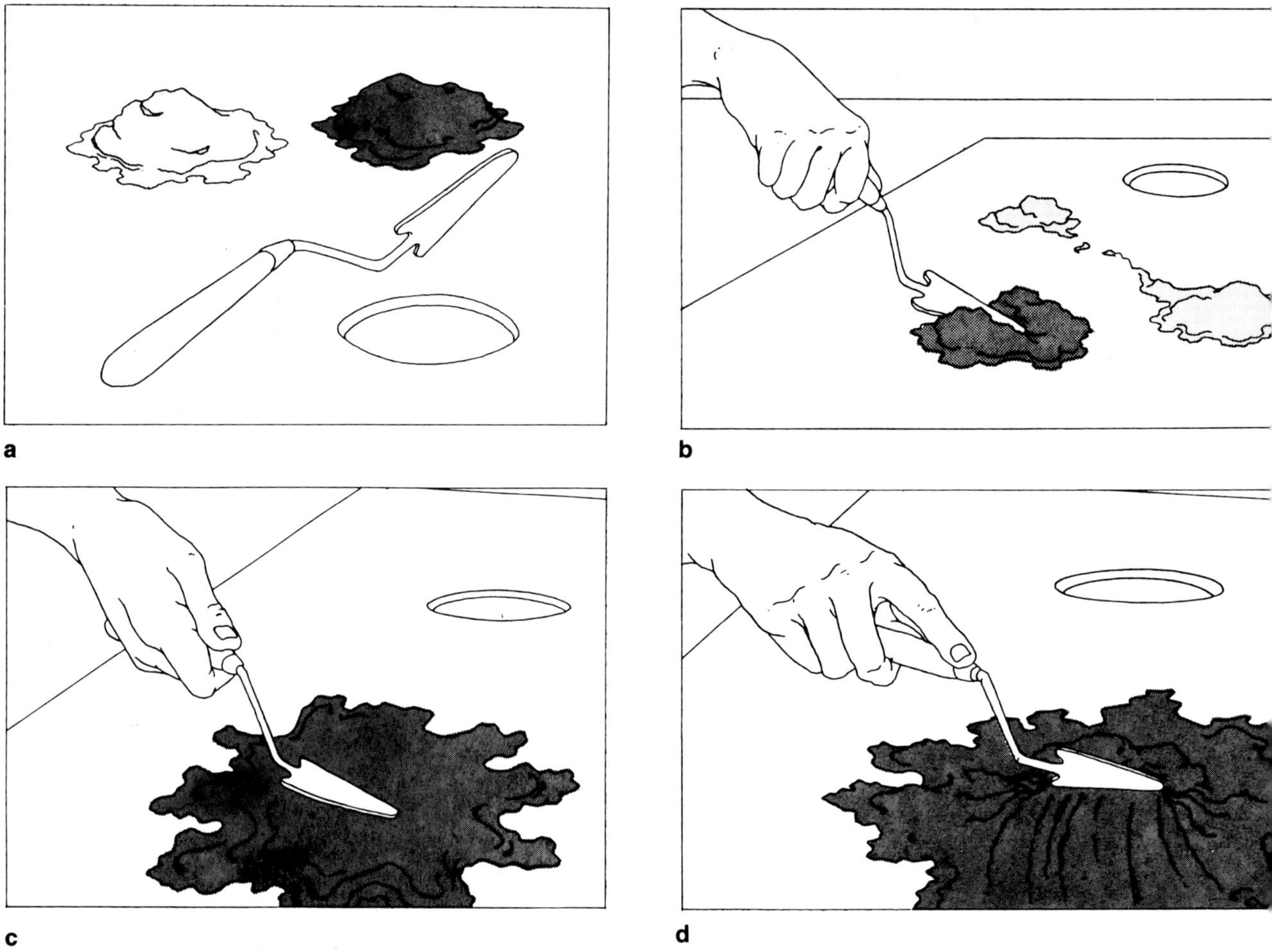

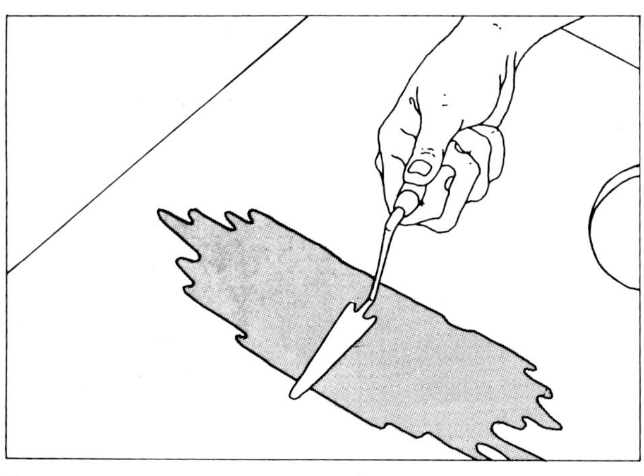

Figure 5-3 (a) Two colors on a clean palette, ready to be mixed. (b) Use just enough of each color to mix the amount of paint you need. (c) Mix the colors thoroughly. (d) Gather the paint on the front or back of the knife (loading the back of the knife like a trowel makes it easier to spread). (e) Spread an even film so that at least a 1- by 3-inch sample may be cut out.

mediate value, a great deal of the light color must be needlessly expended.

Color Matching

A color cannot be matched by verbal description alone. Everyone has an internal concept of each verbal color description that differs significantly from everyone else's, thus making accuracy impossible. The only way to attain a close approximation of another color is to work from a color sample or swatch.

Various notation systems and swatch systems are available on the market today. These not only use descriptive terminology (such as is seen in the Munsell color notation), they also use actual sample colors. A popular and reliable system of color matching is the Pantone system—a marvel in its completeness of paper types, transparent overlays, colored inks and dye markers, and color selectivity in a swatch book. All the colors are coded and matched throughout the system, which greatly simplifies working with printers and other visual arts people when describing a color.

At times, however, using a commercial system is not appropriate. A color may have to be matched in paint in order for the artist to continue work on a canvas or a watercolor; a fabric color may have to be matched in order for the designer/artist to continue work in fiber or on a painted surface for an interior. Any time a paint color needs to be matched for its intrinsic aesthetic value to any other object, the designer/artist must mix and match the new color from a color swatch and produce the match in paint.

Four factors influence one's ability to match a color swatch in paint: the surface(s) involved (glossy, semi-matte, or matte); the grounds involved (the weight and color of the paper, board, or canvas to be used); the colorants used; and the material character of the sample (opaque, transparent, translucent, metallic, or the like).

The simplest, most direct way to match a color is to use the identical materials used in the original swatch. For example, if the color to be matched is brushed in oil paint opaquely on a brown masonite ground and then varnished, it will be very difficult to produce even a reasonably close match using transparent watercolor paint on a white matte board. Imagining that identical situations will always prevail is not realistic, so the question becomes, how can the task be made easier? The way to begin is to make as many factors as possible in creating the match either the same or similar. Suppose that (as often happens) a designer/artist is asked to match a color from a piece of fabric (color swatch) to a paint color in a serigraph that is to hang over a sofa covered in the fabric. The accuracy of the match may seem impossible because the reflective characteristics of the fabric are quite different from the reflective qualities of the paint film. But even if an exact match is not possible, at least two positive circumstances do exist:

1. The two colors will be related as to hue, intensity, and value.
2. The two colors may be lit in the same manner, with the same color temperature of light.

If the room is lit with incandescent lighting, a reflector lamp of the same quality incandescence secured to the frame housing the serigraph or used as a spot in the ceiling will help establish a similar color balance. Distance, too, can help create the illusion that the colors are the same when in fact they are only similar.

Because colorant mixing, as referred to in this section, is confined to matching a color swatch of any material with opaque paint pigment, the use of inks, dyes, colored pencils, pastels, and dye markers serves only to approximate a color match and cannot recreate it, unless the original color swatch is in one of these media.

The following section works with color samples and eye training and involves sensitizing the designer/artist in much the same way that ear training works for a musician. This is a simple, direct method of producing new colors either to serve as short cuts for color matching or to supply organized color for new aesthetic expression. Although it is impossible to store hundreds of color possibilities in one's memory, it is possible to go to a recorded source for new color control. Practice in color discrimination by comparison and exposure to new mixes is essential in developing color sensitivity.

New Vocabularies of Color

One of the best ways to build new vocabularies of color is by means of color modulations or gradual changes from one color to another. Such modulations can be achieved by systematically mixing the two and then making variations on those systems through tinting, toning, and shading. It is thus possible to make hundreds of new colors very simply and, in doing so, to train the eye to color matching as swiftly as possible. The most direct mix will produce the cleanest, closest match. Adding more color than is necessary invariably yields mixtures that are low in intensity and have a muddy appearance.

The four different types of color modulations are complementary, secondary, analogous, and miscellaneous. The procedure for making each type of modulation scale is the same; the mixing technique has already been discussed.

A color modulation is made up of two parent colors or hues that form the outer limits for each scale. The parent colors are mixed in graded proportions to create a progression from one color to the other. The number of offspring or intermediary colors is determined by the designer/artist and by the extent of color information desired. It is possible to produce a very simple modulation of four or five colors, but the most helpful scales for developing color awareness and control contain a dozen or more steps (figure 5-4). Figure 5-5 shows a modulation between two complements, based on different proportions of red and green. Try to develop the habit of recording the brand of paint and the pigments used for a specific modulation. It becomes very clear that one red/green modulation does not always produce the same intermediary colors as another. For this reason, notes or records in a notebook can be a great help in replicating a particular modulation color.

If a modulation produces very dark mixtures

Figure 5-4 A 13-step Modulation Between Cerulean Blue and a Mixture of Cadmium Red Medium and Cadmium Orange (All scales were made with Liquitex acrylic paint.)

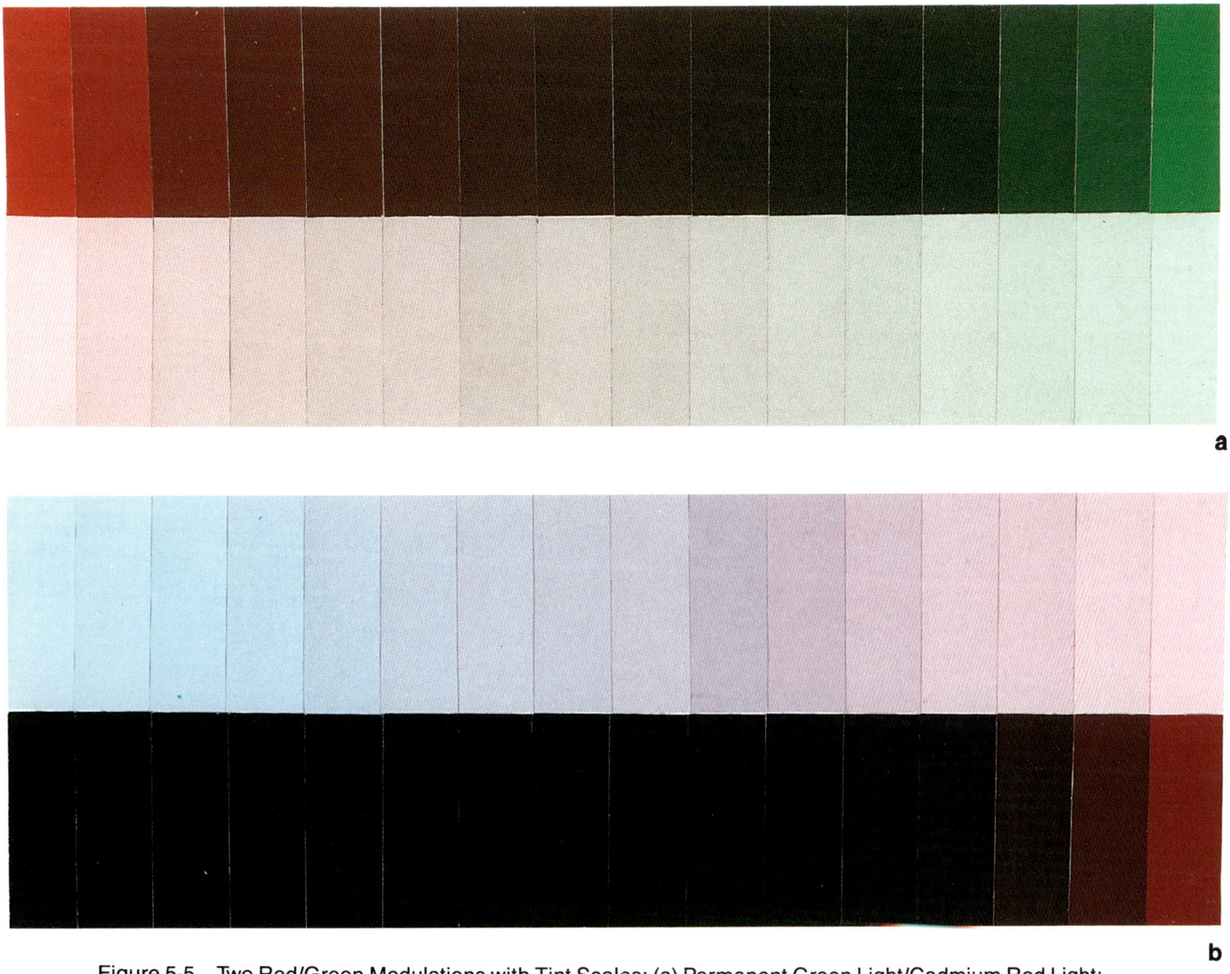

Figure 5-5 Two Red/Green Modulations with Tint Scales: (a) Permanent Green Light/Cadmium Red Light; (b) Phthalocyanine Green/Alizarin Crimson.

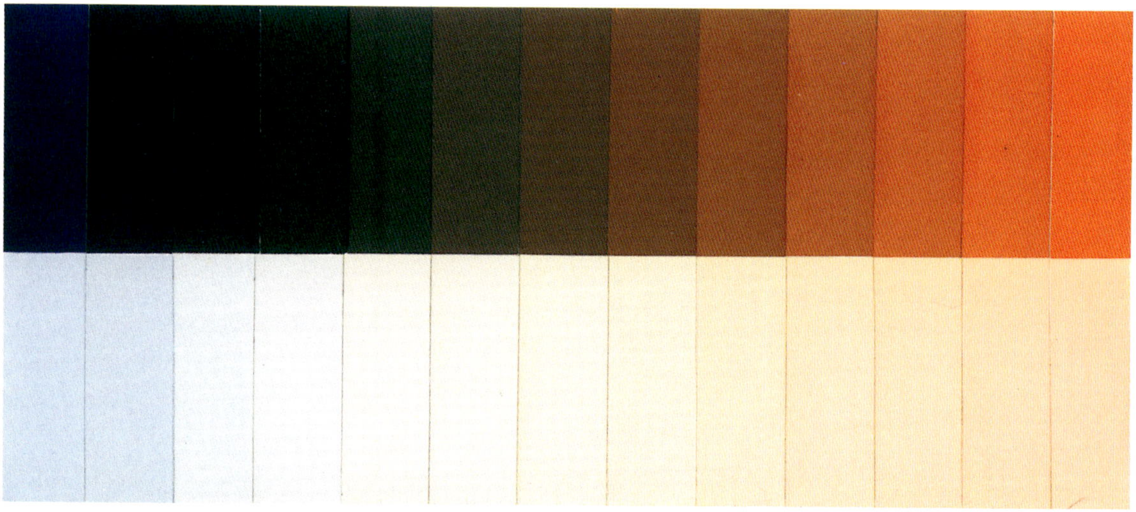

Figure 5-6 Blue/Orange Modulation (Ultramarine Blue/Cadmium Orange), with Tint Scale

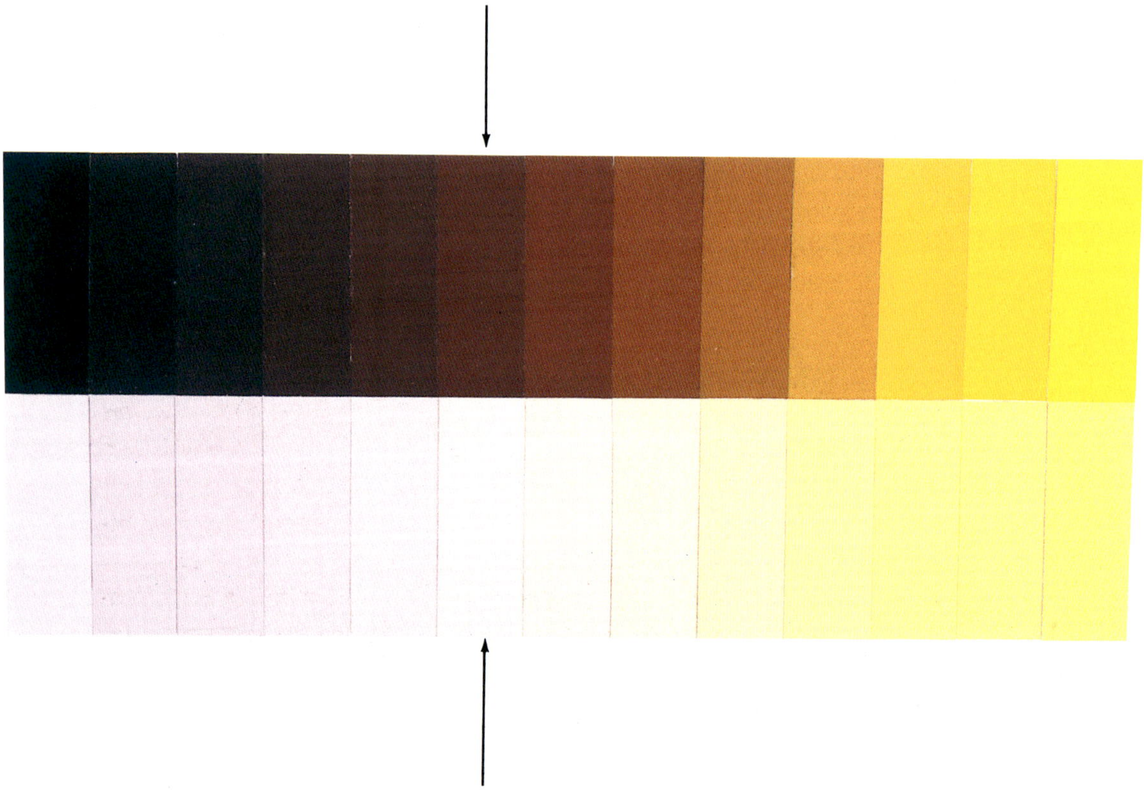

Figure 5-7 Violet/Yellow Modulation (Dioxazine Violet/Cadmium Yellow Light), with Tint Scale Showing Neutral

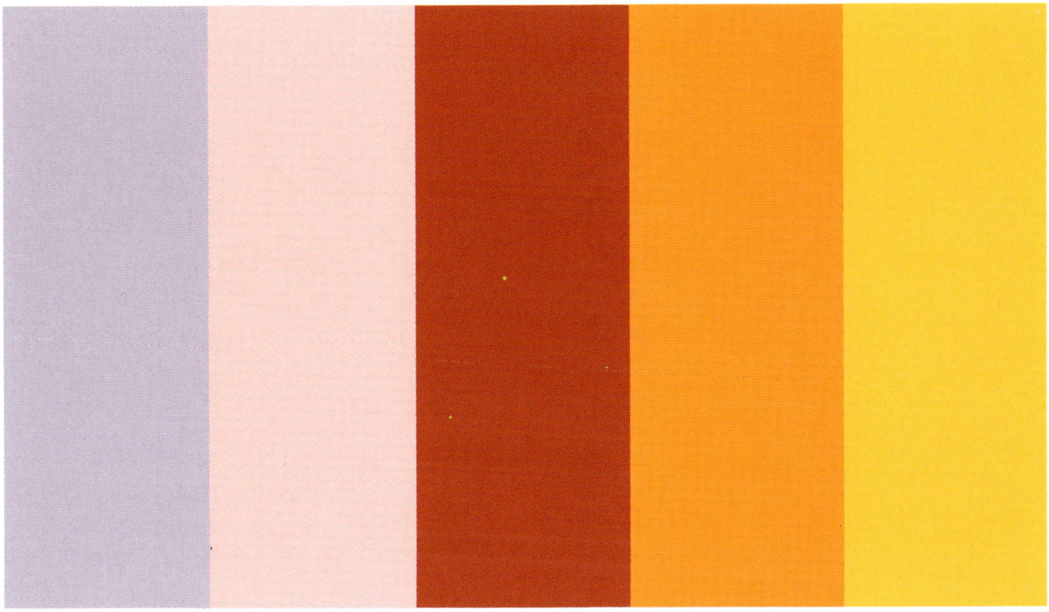

Figure 5-8 Color Unity Produced by Five Colors Selected from a Violet/Yellow Modulation (Cadmium Yellow Medium/Cobalt Violet)

or if the intermediary colors appear very similar, the easiest way of perceiving the gradual color shift is by tinting each color or step as it is produced; producing a tint scale at the same time each step in the original modulation is made saves time and supplies information about the undertone of each new mix. Each tint should be mixed to the same value, however, so that a consistent series of new colors results, without incorporating any misleading value shifts.

The low-intensity colors that lie toward the middle of complementary modulations are beautiful as entities in themselves. These colors, or chromatic neutrals, exhibit temperature changes rather than obvious hue changes (figure 5-6). When two or three of these colors are isolated, it becomes quite apparent that their subtle differences are best expressed in terms of relative warmth or coolness. It also becomes clear that lying somewhere amongst these chromatic neutrals is a true neutral in temperature, as well. The true neutral for a particular pair of complements exists when all wavelengths of light are absorbed and little or no selective reflection occurs (figure 5-7).

The number of new colors that can be produced by complementary modulation is a challenge in itself. For example, a 24-hue circle contains 12 pairs of complements. If each set is mixed to a modulation of 15 steps, 180 new colors will be produced. Each scale may be tinted, toned, or shaded, which adds up to

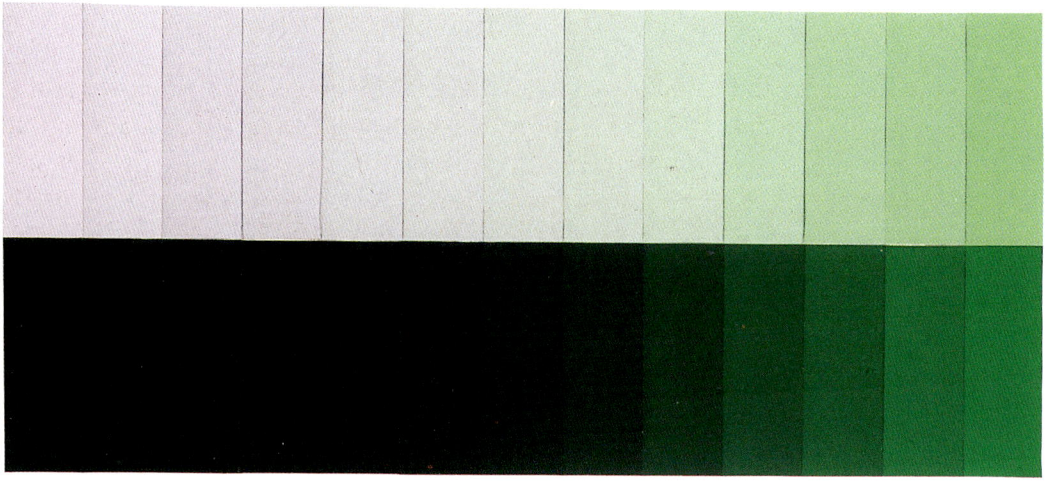

Figure 5-9 Violet/Green Secondary Modulation Showing a Dominance of Blue (Permanent Green Light/Dioxazine Violet)

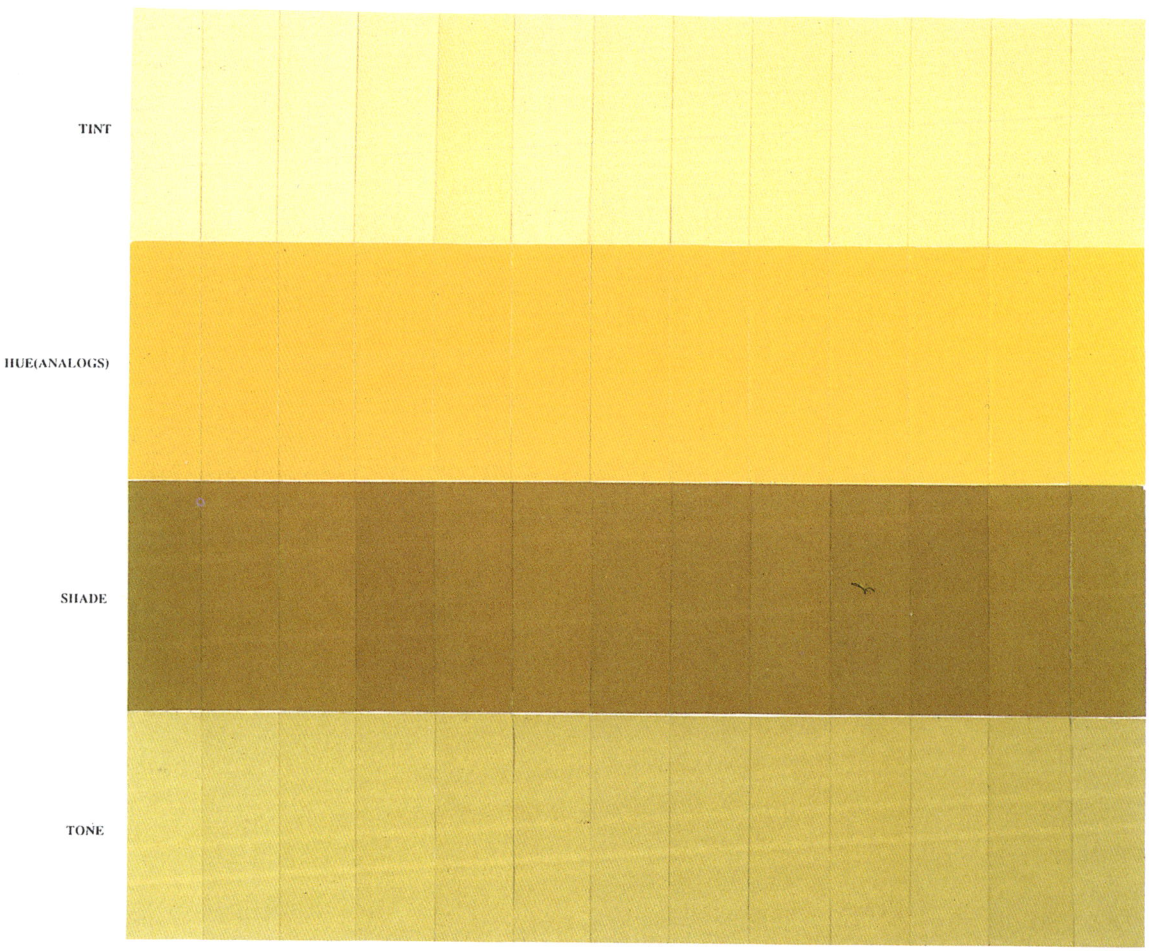

an additional 540 colors. Thus, 720 colors can be produced from an original set of 12 pairs of complements.

An excellent method for controlling color in a work is by limiting the palette to a minimum of values and therefore a minimum of hues or colors. As was pointed out in Chapter 4, simultaneity is a simple way to make a few values and hues/colors seem to multiply the total number of colors present. The eye/brain, meanwhile, does not become confused and reads the design with greater ease and comprehension. For example, if five values are used and those in turn are translated into colors from a single modulation, the color unity—that is, the sense of wholeness or connectedness—becomes very strong. Even though the colors appear to be different (figure 5-8), there is a subtle connection that the viewer recognizes subliminally.

Another system of modulation produces colors by mixing secondary colors—orange plus green, green plus violet, or violet plus orange. The resulting colors are called tertiary mixtures, because they are made up of all three primaries in varying degrees. Unlike complementary mixtures (which also consist of all three primaries but produce a neutral color), however, the secondary modulations do not produce neutrals; there is always a dominance of red, yellow, or blue (figure 5-9). Analyzing the combinations reveals why these dominances exist. When orange and green are mixed, the components are red + *yellow* + blue + *yellow*. Yellow is the dominant primary running through this modulation. When green and violet are mixed, the mixture breaks down to *blue* + yellow + *blue* + red; thus, the dominant primary here is blue. When orange and violet are modulated, the dominance is red. All of the colors produced by secondary modulations resemble colors found in nature: the reds of the sky at dusk and dawn, the blues of beach stones and marine creatures, and the yellow-browns of dried grasses and leaves in late summer and early fall. The nuances are endless.

Analogous modulations are neither as dramatic nor as varied as complementary and secondary ones. They are basically scales between two hues or related colors (figure 5-10). More variation occurs when these scales are tinted, shaded, or toned and then used in conjunction with their hues. Spatial effects are easily achieved when such relationships are established.

Miscellaneous modulations may be made between two earth colors—siennas, umbers, ochres, synthetic iron oxides, or others. The undertones and intermediary colors found in such modulations, when used in conjunction with the parent colors, often possess unexpected richness. The tints especially have surprising qualities. Consequently, producing such scales, even in a few steps, can be very satisfying. Other pigments that offer varying results are modulations done with metallics, Day-Glo, or fluorescent colors. These can lead to surprising combinations and are suggested for colorists who like to experiment.

Two techniques can be used to enhance color in general: glazes and scumbles. Glaz-

Figure 5-10 Analogous Modulation Between Yellow and Yellow-Orange-Yellow (Cadmium Yellow Light/Cadmium Yellow Medium) Showing Tint, Hue, Shade, and tint of Shade Scales ing imparts a thin, transparent film of color over a preexisting one. The procedure is as simple as combining a thin mixture of a pigment with any water-based paint, or diluting oil color in linseed oil with a small amount of varnish. These glazes may be used as an underpainting or an overpainting for another color. Multiple glazes may be built up, with each being allowed to dry between applications, so that deep, rich color is achieved. Scumbling is a semiopaque glaze that can be used to create a translucent feeling in clouds and smoke; unfortunately its use is limited.

To control color is to understand it. An enriching, creative experience in which the intellect merges with the intuition can only happen when a solid base of knowledge already exists.

6 STUDIO PROJECTS

The following projects are based on the information in Chapters 1 through 5. While answers to specific questions are found in the body of the text, these exercises are open to interpretation, style, taste, and the needs of the individual designer/artist. Although methods and techniques are suggested, the projects may be in any medium that seems appropriate—paint, paper, ink, colored pencil, pastel, dye, fiber, collage, photography, light, and so on.

Chapter 1

1. Fabricate an additive-mixing hue circle showing the relationship between primary and secondary hues.
2. Using pigment, approximate the light mixtures that result when a primary light hue is mixed with a secondary light hue, i.e., either its complement or its analog.
3. Note the difference between a pigment, ink, and dye and make samples of each.
4. In pigment, ink, or dye show how the magenta of the light hue circle is produced.
5. Select filters (acetate gels) which simulate the colors of the true subtractive primaries, i.e., those primaries that produce black in reflected color, and demonstrate with a single light source why they are called subtractive.
6. Analyze and demonstrate the subtractive nature of a paint mixture of (a) yellow/orange and (b) yellow/blue.
7. What are the three conditions that influence the nature of a reflected color? Illustrate using any medium you wish.
8. Place two different surface samples of the same color (for example, two samples of fiber, one silk, one wool) or two different samples of a painted surface (such as a matte and a gloss) and light them with a single light source. Is there any difference in the color quality?
9. Make two identical color cards by placing four 2-inch squares of colored paper using red, orange, blue and green on an 11- by 14-inch piece of gray illustration board or mat board. Next, place each card under a different light source, i.e., one incandescent, the other fluorescent, and observe them simultaneously. What are the differences?

10. Take a single object with an intense color from daylight illumination into a dimly lit room. How does the color change?

Chapter 2

1. What are the four basic properties of reflected color? Illustrate using any medium you wish.
2. In any subtractive medium, or with paper or fabric, produce a hue circle based on (a) the RYB system and (b) the MYC system. Use only the primaries and secondaries of each system.
3. Produce two hue circles using the RYB and MYC systems which include only the six central intermediary hues (for example, the RYB system would include, YO, RO, RV, BV, BG, and GY).
4. Execute a value scale of at least fifteen steps in any medium, keeping the progression from black to white as even in gradation as possible. (If you choose paint, please refer to Chapter 5.)
5. Produce a design in one of the major value keys (use value only).
6. Repeat Exercise 5 in a minor key.
7. To compare value and intensity: (a) Make a tint scale of at least six steps from hue to white (refer to Chapter 5 for paint mixing). Consider the hue as 100-percent saturated, or fully intense, decreasing to the value which contains no colorant and is 0 percent. (b) Make a shade scale from the hue to black. (c) Make a tone scale from the hue to its relative value.
8. In any paint medium, add a small amount of any intense violet, i.e., cobalt or dioxidine violet to a larger amount of yellow. Mix thoroughly. Now reverse the process, adding a small amount of yellow to violet, and note the difference in tinctorial power between the two colors.
9. It is suggested that this exercise first be done in any paint medium. When the colors are established, repeat with paper, found objects, fabric, etc., by duplicating the color. Make three mixtures of cadmium red medium, cobalt blue, and cadmium yellow so that each mixture has a color quality that leans toward one of the primaries, i.e., in one mixture the cadmium red medium will appear to dominate. Note that the tinctorial strength of each color is different, and does not necessarily reflect the amount of paint added to the mixture.
10. Certain colors and their corresponding temperatures may be ascribed to different emotions; for example, red may be used to symbolize anger or passion or love; green for envy or jealousy; etc. List as many emotions as possible and the color or colors, used in combination, that seem to correspond with each. This will be subjective to some extent, depending on the cultural background of the designer/artist. However

it does become evident that certain colors are viewed the same way by a majority of people within a culture.

Chapter 3

1. With a hole puncher place holes as close to the center of each step of the value scale made in Exercise 4 for Chapter 2. Next select a variety of solid colors from magazines and/or colored papers such as Color Aid or Pantone and find their relative values.
2. Translate a value design from any source into color.
3. Translate a major and a minor value key design of your own into color.
4. Lower the intensity of a single hue in five different ways.
5. (a) Compare the undertones of two greens by tinting out *permanent green light* and *viridian* or *pthalocyanine green*. (b) Make a simple design or painting using only tints of approximately 30 percent (value) of two reds and two blues. Notice how the temperature change evokes very subtle changes in the illusion of space. Warm colors, even as tints, tend to advance; cool colors recede.
6. Execute a design or painting using two hues of the same value with tints and shades of each hue. Besides the hues, limit the number of tints and shades to two of each hue.
7. Execute a design or painting using two hues of different values as well as tints of two shades/hues.
8. Find illustrations from magazines or reproductions that utilize the contrast of complementary colors. Make a list of those found. The hue circle is a good reference tool.
9. Select two of Goethe's harmonious ratios—for example, yellow/violet 1:3 and orange/blue 1:2, and execute a design or painting using just these hues.
10. Using Exercise 9, translate the design or painting into tints and see if the ratios need to be changed in order to produce a visual balance.

Chapter 4

1. Create a color pattern which, when you look successively at it and then a white board, produces (a) a strong hue afterimage and (b) a weak hue afterimage.
2. Create a value pattern which, when you look successively at it and then a gray board produces (a) a strong value afterimage and (b) a weak value afterimage.
3. Using successive contrast and a white ground discover the afterimage effect of a compound hue such as yellow-green, or yellow-green-yellow. Try it again using a gray ground and then a black ground, and note how these background values change the quality of the afterimage.
4. Execute a design using a black back-

ground with foreground shapes of intense color/hue.

5. Recreate Exercise 4 on a white background keeping the foreground colors/hues exactly the same.
6. Recreate Exercise 4 on a middle gray background, again keeping the foreground colors exactly the same. Place Exercises 4, 5, and 6 side by side and note the apparent differences in the foreground colors/hues.
7. On a piece of gray mat board place a 4- × 4-inch square of black paper and a 4- × 4-inch square of white paper side by side. Use rubber cement to mount the papers. Next place a 1- × 1-inch square of the same middle value in the center of each large square. One single value now has the appearance of two separate values. Run a 1/4-inch strip of the value used across the bottom of both large squares to show that the center squares are indeed the same value.
8. Using the same technique as in Exercise 7, create the illusion that two values that are approximately 35 percent and 50 percent look similar. Keep the backgrounds black and white; the high contrast produces the most dramatic effect. See if other values can be made to look similar by using different value backgrounds. The closer in value the background squares become, the closer in value the foreground squares will also have to be to keep the illusion of similarity.
9. Using the technique in Exercise 7 show apparent changes in intensity by using the same color foreground square on background squares that are (a) the same family as the foreground, but of different value and intensity and (b) complementary to the foreground square.
10. Make two small squares of the same high value and place them on (a) a background of a tint of a similar color (for example, a 10 percent tint of red on a 10 percent tint of orange) and (b) a background of a tint of a complementary color (for example, a 10 percent tint of red on a 10 percent tint of blue) and compare the results.

Chapter 5

1. Assemble the painting equipment necessary to mix paint samples using the technique described in the text. Practice mixing values by experimenting with the tinctorial strengths of (a) mars black mixed with white and (b) ivory black mixed with white. Take each tint scale from black to white with a minimum of six steps. Is there a different undertone for each black, or are they very similar?
2. Compare a 10 percent value swatch of each black.
3. Make a shade scale of (a) mars black and cadmium yellow light and (b) mars black and cadmium yellow medium. Repeat the scales using ivory black. Keeping the values of each of the steps similar, compare the first and second

shades of all four mixes. How do they compare in color quality?

4. Choose two of the darkest shades from Exercise 3 and tint them to approximately 30 percent. Compare the tints of the shades with straight tints of each color. What is the difference in color quality?
5. Produce a twelve-step modulaton including a tint scale of the complementary pairs (a) ultramarine blue and cadmium orange and (b) cerulean blue and cadmium orange.
6. Find the color and its tint on each modulation of Exercise 5 that appears to be the neutral for that modulation, i.e., the color that by comparison to its neighbors is neither warm nor cool but falls in between. Next compare the two neutrals of each complementary mix side by side.
7. Execute a design or painting using five colors from a modulation without using either parent color.
8. Produce a five-step scale of any tube color(s) of the following: (a) a tint scale, (b) a shade scale, (c) a tone scale, (d) a tint of a shade scale. Create a design, pattern, or painting using at least one color from each scale.
9. Match two color swatches of any material(s) as closely as possible with paint, ink, or dye.
10. Selecting no more than five colors from any or all of the secondary modulations, produce a design or painting. Work out the value organization first and use white and black if a major key is chosen.

INDEX

ABOUT THE AUTHOR

Patricia Lambert teaches color and two-dimensional design at the Parsons School of Design and the New School in New York City. An accomplished artist and photographer, she has exhibited across the U.S. and abroad, and she frequently lectures and conducts workshops on color theory and application for the fine artist and craftsperson. Her articles on color have appeared in a number of trade publications, and she is coauthor of *Color and Fiber,* an authoritative study.

OTHER BOOKS FROM DESIGN PRESS